SIR

CHARLES HENRY FRANKLAND,

BARONET:

OR

BOSTON IN THE COLONIAL TIMES.

BY

ELIAS NASON, M. A.

> Time rolls his ceaseless course. The race of yore,
> Who danced our infancy upon their knee,
> And told our marvelling boyhood legends store,
> Of their strange ventures happ'd by land or sea,
> How are they blotted from the things that be.
>
> SIR WALTER SCOTT.

ALBANY, N. Y.:
J. MUNSELL, 78 STATE STREET.
1865.

PREFACE.

"Who was Sir Charles Henry Frankland?" is a question which a brief story, entitled a *Legend of New England*, and published by William Lincoln, Esq., in 1843; and, still more recently, the ballad of *Agnes*, by Dr. Oliver Wendell Holmes, have led the public to entertain. Was he a real personage or a myth; was there ever such a collector of the port of Boston; was he, indeed, buried under the ruins of Lisbon at the time of the great earthquake; was he rescued therefrom by the efforts of a poor girl named Agnes Surriage; did he afterwards make her his wife?

Is the legend true, or but the wild figment of some romancing brain? Only scattered fragments of colonial history are extant; how then shall we determine who this Sir Charles Henry Frankland was?

This very natural question I have endeavored to answer in the following pages.

It was my fortune to spend several of the happiest

years of my boyhood at the Frankland Place, in Hopkinton, Massachusetts; to see some few of the fast-fading memorials of Sir Charles Henry and Lady Agnes Frankland; to gather fruit and flowers from the trees and shrubberies which they had planted, and especially, to hear from the lips of Mrs. Mary Hildreth,—a lady of unusual force of mind, whose former husband, Dr. T. Shepherd, received the place from Mrs. Swain as early as 1793,—the Rev. Nathaniel Howe, Matthew Metcalf, Esq., Gilbert Dench Wilson, and others who had been well acquainted with a brother and sister of Lady Frankland, or their children, the romantic story of the visit to Marblehead, the rescue of the knight by Agnes Surriage from death at Lisbon, and other incidents connected with their eventful life at Hopkinton and Boston. At that period, indeed, some of the negro servants of Mrs. Swain, a sister of Lady Frankland, were still living, and a few aged persons, as Madam Elizabeth Price, who could well remember Sir Harry himself.

These remarkable stories, associated, as they were, with the old mansion and the wild and picturesque domain once occupied by the Indians, made a vivid impression upon my imagination, and I afterwards determined to verify them as opportunity might occur, and commit them to writing.

In doing this, I have examined many manuscript and printed pages, and files of colonial newspapers; I have fallen unexpectedly upon Sir Henry's Journal,—written in his own hand and covering a period of about thirteen years,—and have also received assistance and letters of encouragement from many different individuals, among whom I would most gratefully mention my very learned antiquarian friend, S. G. Drake, Esq.; the Rev. Alfred L. Baury; Dr. Oliver W. Holmes, whose charming ballad of *Agnes*, breathes the very spirit of the colonial times; Miss T. T. Whinyates, of Cheltenham, England, descendant of Sir Thomas Frankland, fifth Baronet, and Mrs. Lydia T. [Ellis] Dawes, to whose father, Josiah Ellis, Esq., Edward Surriage sold the Frankland mansion at Boston in 1811.

If my researches serve in any way to answer the question, "Who was Sir Charles Henry Frankland?" or to exhibit life as it was in Boston under the old colonial regime, which the blood of our honored fathers washed away, they may not, as I hope, have been vainly undertaken.

January 1, 1865.

CHARLES HENRY FRANKLAND.

CHAPTER I.

Birth of Frankland — Parentage — Family — Education — Companions — His father's death — Appointed Collector of the Port of Boston.

SIR CHARLES HENRY FRANKLAND, whose eventful history I now purpose to relate, was a lineal descendant of Oliver Cromwell,[1] Lord Protector of

[1] Pedigree of the Frankland family from Cromwell to the present time. Oliver Cromwell, Lord Protector, b. 1599 d. 1658, m. Elizabeth, daughter of Sir James Bouchier of Folsted, Essex. The youngest daughter, Frances Cromwell, m. first, the Hon. Robert Rich, who d. 1657, and second, Sir John Russell of Cheltenham, Bart. Sir Thomas Frankland of Thirkleby, 2d Bart., m. Elizabeth Russell. She d. 1733. His eldest son, Thomas, succeeded him as 3d baronet. Henry Frankland, fourth son of the 2d baronet, Governor of the Hon. East India Co's Factory, Bengal, m. Elizabeth Cross, daughter of Alexr. Cross, Esq., merchant, and had seven sons and three daughters. Sir CHARLES HENRY FRANKLAND, 4th Bart., oldest son of the above, m. Miss Agnes Surriage of New England. Sir Thomas Frankland, 5th Bart., Admiral of the White and brother of the above, m. Miss Sarah Rhett of South Carolina. Sir Thomas Frankland, 6th Bart., (b. 1750, d. 1820,) m. Miss Dorothy Smelt, daughter of William Smelt, Esq., of Yorkshire. Sir Robert Frankland, 7th Bart., took the name of Russell in addition to his own. He m. Miss Louisa Murray, youngest daughter of the Hon. and Rev. Lord George Murray, Bishop of St. Davids. Sir Frederick Frankland, the 8th and present Bart., succeeded his cousin in 1849. He m. Miss Scaith of Yorkshire.—(From Miss Whinyates, of Cheltenham, Eng.)

England, and was born in Bengal on the tenth day of May, 1716. His family is one of the most ancient, wealthy and respectable in the north of England. The very name Frankland[1] itself would indicate a remarkable antiquity, that being the appellation which was given in feudal times to the original proprietor of the soil. The seat of the family is Great Thirkleby Hall at Thirsk,[2] in the north riding of Yorkshire, England.

The title of baronet was conferred on WILLIAM FRANKLAND, the head of the family, by Charles the Second in 1660. His son, Sir THOMAS FRANKLAND, the second baronet, married Elizabeth, daughter of Sir John and Lady Frances Russell, the youngest and favorite child of Cromwell, and whose personal attractions were such as to lead Charles the Second to solicit her hand in marriage.[3] Henry, the fourth son of Sir Thomas Frankland, resided at Mattersea, in Nottinghamshire, and married Elizabeth, daugh-

---

[1] The coat of arms is, Azure, a dolphin naiant, embowed, or on a chief of the second, two saltiers, gules. Crest on a wreath, a dolphin argent, haurient and entwined round an anchor, proper. The motto is beautiful and significant;—"Libera terra: liberque animus,"—that is, Free soil and free soul. See Burke's *Peerage and Baronetcy of the British Empire.* See Dr. Franklin's *Autobiography*, p. 6, who derives his name from the same source.

[2] This town contains about 3000 people. It is delightfully situated on the banks of the river Colleck, over which are thrown two elegant stone bridges. The church is Gothic, and the ruins of an immense castle, built by the Mowbrays in 979, give a melancholy interest to the place.

[3] "Charles II was for marrying her." See Carlyle's *Cromwell*, vol. I, p. 67.

ter of Alexander Cross, Esq., by whom he had seven sons, the oldest of whom was CHARLES HENRY, who was born while his father was residing abroad as governor of the East India company's factory at Bengal.[1]

CHARLES HENRY FRANKLAND was educated in affluence and as the presumptive heir to the baronetcy and the estates at Thirkleby and Mattersea. Of his early days I have been able to glean but few memorials; yet it appears that the culture of his mind and manners was by no means neglected. He acquired a competent knowledge of the French and Latin languages; and what is better still, the art of using his own with ease and elegance. He studied with diligence the political and literary history of his own country, and made himself familiar with the principles of natural science, so far as then understood. Botany and landscape-gardening afforded him most delightful recreation, and occupied many of his leisure moments, even till the very close of life. His intellectual attainments fitted him for the society of such men as Horace Walpole, but one year younger than himself,—Henry Fielding, his senior by eleven years; and

[1] The other children of Henry Frankland were: I. Thomas, who succeeded his brother Charles Henry as baronet in 1768, and d. at Bath Nov. 21, 1784: II, William, b. 1721: III. Frederick app. Comptroller of the duties of the excise in Feb. 1763: IV. Ann, who m. Thomas Pelham 1st Earl of Chichester: V. Robert, captain of the Yarmouth, and barbarously murdered by the natives of Judda: VI. Mary, who m. Thomas Worsley, Esq: VII. Frances, who m. Roger Talbot, Esq.

the earl of Chesterfield, whom he is said to have resembled both in his manners and his person.

By the death of his father at Bengal, in 1738, he came, at the early age of twenty-two, into the possession of an ample fortune, and the noble and extensive alliances of his family gave him such influence at the court of George the Second, that when two of the most honorable offices in the American colonies, the governorship of Massachusetts, and the collectorship of the port of Boston, became vacant by the removal of Jonathan Belcher[1] and the death of John Jekyl, the choice of these royal favors was offered by the duke of Newcastle, then secretary of the southern department of colonial affairs, to Mr. Frankland.[2]

Sir William Shirley[3] a lawyer, who had resided seven years in Boston, desired the office of collector

---

[1] "Accused of complicity with Dr. Cutler and the Rev. Commissary Price to ruin the dissenting interest." *Douglas*, vol. I, p. 482.

[2] His uncle, Sir Thomas Frankland, was one of the Lords of the Admiralty in 1741.

[3] William Shirley was born in England 1693; came to this country about 1734, and was Gov. of Mass. from 1741 to 1756. He m. for his first wife, Miss Frances Baker of London, a lady of great personal attractions, by whom he had I. William, killed under Braddock 1755; II. John, who d. a captain in the army: III. Thomas, created Bart. 1786: IV. Elizabeth, who m. Eliakim Hutchinson; V. Frances, who m. Wm. Bollan, Esq.: VI. Harriet, who m. Robert Temple, Esq.; VII. Maria, who m. John Erving, Esq. Gov. Shirley built the spacious mansion in Roxbury, afterwards occupied by Gov. Wm. Eustis, and d. there in 1771. He published *Electra, a Tragedy*, 1765, and also *Hercules, a Masque*. "He was a man of prudence and sagacity."—*Hildreth*.

as more lucrative; and his beautiful and accomplished Lady Frances, being then in London, used her influence at court to obtain it for him, but "a strong interest," says Hutchinson, "being made for Mr. Frankland, since Sir Henry Frankland, there was no way of providing for both, except by giving the government to Mr Shirley.[1]"

[1]See Hutchinson's *History of Mass.*, vol., II, p. 358.

CHAPTER II.

Frankland and Shirley contrasted — Aristocratic spirit of the times — Manners and customs — Literature — Dress — Deference to Crown officers — Undercurrent of republican sentiment — Portrait of Frankland — Peter Fanueil — Boston at this period — Newspapers.

FRANKLAND and Shirley entered on their respective offices in 1741; they were both well born and well educated; they were both ardent lovers of the fatherland; they were both, of course, Episcopalians and worshipped side by side at the King's chapel under commissary Roger Price; they had the polished manners of the days of Bolingbroke and Chesterfield; they were wealthy, generous, ambitious, and for a time they moved as "the bright particular stars" in that refined and aristocratic circle, embracing the Amorys,[1] Apthorps, Bollans,[2] Hutchin-

[1] There were three brothers Amory in Boston at this period,— Thomas, b, 1722, Jonathan, b. 1726, and John, b. 1728. They were well educated, wealthy, and respectable. See *Gen. Reg.*, January, 1856.

[2] William Bollan, Esq., came to this country a little prior to the arrival of Frankland, and was collector of Salem and Marblehead. He obtained £175,000 from England, in 1748, as reimbursement to the state for the expense of the expedition against Cape Breton. He was an able lawyer, and left several valuable political tracts. Died in England 1776. See Hutchinson's *Hist. Mass.* vol. II, p. 436.

sons,[1] Prices, Auchmutys, Overings, Chardons, Wendells, Olivers, etc., who held the money, offices and power, and represented the court of St. James in Boston at that remarkable period; and in the public life of the one, developing and leading the colonial forces to a successful contest with the aggressive power of France upon our frontiers; and in the private life of the other, chequered as a poet's dream, we have the full embodiment of the practical and romantic spirit of that ante-revolutionary period. Though an aspiration after civil liberty had been awakened among the people, and the fire was slowly kindling on her sacred altar, the city of Boston was still the servile imitator of the fashions and the follies of the mother country. The principal offices of state were filled by men of influence from abroad who, with their families and dependents, took the precedence in society and laid down laws for its observance. "How is this done at court?" was the question of the day; and who could answer it so well as those just from the court — the people very naturally concluded; and so they listened and yielded to the voice of their transatlantic leaders. The same aristocratic distinction between families, the

---

[1] Hutchinson, Thomas, grad. H. U. 1727, and Governor of Mass. 1771-1774. His *History of the Province of Mass. Bay*, from 1628 to 1774 is invaluable; but he failed to see or to acknowledge the real principles of American liberty, and therefore became extremely obnoxious to the people. Superseded by Gen. Gage, he sailed for England, June 1774, and died at Brompton June 3, 1780, aet. 68. There is a good account of him in Allen's *Biog. Dict.* See also *N. A. Rev.* No. 38, p. 134-158.

same modes of dress and address, the same courtly manners prevailed here as in London. Those gentlemen and ladies who occupied the north, or court end of the town, who read the *Spectator*, Samuel Richardson's *Pamela*,[1] and the prayer book, who had manors of a thousand acres in the country, cultivated by slaves from Africa, and who were led in their devotions at King's chapel by a Price, a Caner, a Brockwell, or a Troutbeck,[2] were many of them allied to the first families in England and bred at court, and it was their chief ambition to keep up the ceremonies and the customs of the aristocratic society which they represented. They were successful. It is hardly possible for us in these days of republican simplicity to conceive what

---

1 First published 1741.

2 The Rev. John Troutbeck came to Boston in 1755, and succeeded the Rev. Charles Brockwell, [d. Aug. 20, 1755,] as assistant to the Rev. H. Caner, rector of King's chapel. He m. Sarah, daugh. of John Gould, Esq., distiller, by whom he had two daughters: Hannah, b. at Boston, Oct. 1, 1768, m. Wm. Bowes, Esq., and d. in Eng. Jan. 14, 1851; and Sarah, who d. July 1, 1846. Mr. T. was living and preaching at Hopkinton prior to induction to his office at King's chapel. Under date of Jan. 23, 1755, he writes from this town to Rev. Roger Price, who had invited him to act as his attorney: "I am far from thinking Hopkinton the paradise it was described to be; but, however, I shall not complain of it if I can have my health in it." He was appointed chaplain to the Rose frigate, 1769, but continued to officiate at King's chapel till 1775, when he left for Halifax, and sometime afterwards for England, where he died. His property was confiscated. His widow returned to this country and lived at Hingham, where she d. Aug. 1813, aged 77, and was buried under King's chapel. See *Gen. Reg.* Jan. 1857, p. 96. Also Sprague's *Annals of American Pulpit*, vol. V, art. Price.

distinction title, blood, escutcheon, family, in that regime conferred. A baronet was then approached with greatest deference; a coach and four with an armorial bearing and liveried servants was a munition against indignity; the stamp of the crown upon a piece of paper, even, invested it with an association almost sacred. In those dignitaries,— who, in brocade vest, goldlace coat, broad ruffled sleeves and small clothes; who with three-cornered hat and powdered wig, side arms and silver shoe buckles, promenaded Queen street[1] and the Mall, spread themselves through the King's chapel, or discussed the measures of the Pelhams, Walpole, and Pitt, at the Rose and Crown, one century and a quarter ago,—as much of aristocratic pride, as much of courtly consequence displayed itself, as in the frequenters of Hyde park, or Regent street, and so it held until we learned from Franklin, Adams, Otis, Hancock, and their compeers, in the grand social and political upheaving of 1776, the magnificent republican lesson so well expressed by Robert Burns:

> "The rank is but the guinea's stamp,
> The man's the gowd for a' that."

Such was the state of society in Boston when Frankland, an accomplished, wealthy and high-bred young man of twenty-four, entered it as collector of the revenue. A picture in my possession, taken about this time, represents him as having a refined and noble cast of features with a peculiarly pensive

[1] Changed to Court street in 1784.

and melancholy expression. The countenance and dress indicate a certain indefinable sweetness of temper and delicacy of taste, such as often characterise those born of English parents in the east. They reveal a mental constitution better adapted to the genial pursuits of literature and art than to the sharp, angular turns of politics or trade.

At the time of his arrival, Boston contained about 16,000 inhabitants, of whom 1514 were negroes. It had at one time during that year 40 top-sail vessels on the stocks, and its commerce outrivalled that of any other town of the English colonies in America. Some 600 ships had been freighted in a year for foreign ports, and the town was rapidly advancing in wealth and refinement. It had ten churches, a handsome town house, a province house, and Peter Faneuil, Esq.,[1] was then erecting, at his own expense, a commodious market and hall for the benefit of the public, to which the name of its munificent founder was immediately given. "The conversation in this town," says John Oldmixon, "is as polite as in most of the towns and cities in England," and "a gentleman from London," he continues, "would almost think himself at home when he observes the number of people, their houses, their furniture, their tables, their dress and conversation." The number of newspapers published here at this time, viz., the *Boston News-Letter*, begun in 1704, the *Boston Gazette*, in 1719, the *Boston Weekly Post-Boy*, in 1734, the *Boston Evening Post*, in 1735, and

[1] Died suddenly, March 3, 1743, at the age of 42 and about 9 mos.

the *New England Weekly Journal*, in 1741, affords conclusive evidence of the intelligence and prosperity of the people. Even then the town was worthy of the name it now so justly bears — The Athens of America.

CHAPTER III.

Collectors — Edward Randolph — His arrest — William Brenton — John Jekyll — Father and son — Management of the revenues.

As the papers of the colonial custom house were destroyed during the revolution, our knowledge of its history is extremely limited. The first royal collector was the celebrated Edward Randolph. Encroaching gradually upon the charter of Massachusetts, the arbitrary and misguided Charles the Second commissioned this gentleman as "collector and searcher and surveyor," of New England, in 1681; and on arriving in Boston, the royal collector notified the people by an advertisement posted in the town house of the establishment of his office. This was torn down by the direction of the general court and the most strenuous efforts made to prevent him from executing his commission. He was an Episcopalian,[1] zealous, arrogant, fearless; and by his efficient labors succeeded in establishing the first Episcopal church in Boston. This activity on behalf of the church of England, whose advent was so intensely dreaded by the Puritans, together with the part he took in causing the abrogation of the charter of the colony in 1684, and the persistent execu-

[1] See *Hist. King's Chapel*, p. 43.

tion of the duties of his office as collector of the revenues, rendered Edward Randolph so obnoxious to the citizens of Boston, that they called him "the myrmidon of a tyrant," and on the reception of the news of the revolution which placed William and Mary upon the throne in 1688, arrested him, together with Sir Edmund Andros, Benjamin Bullivant and others, immured them in prison, and in the beginning of the next year sent them over to England. Randolph was succeeded in the custom house, then called the *naval office*, by William Brenton, Esq., who arrived in Boston with Mr. Dudley, just appointed chief justice of New York, on the 24th of January 1691, and continued in office, acceptably to the people—though he was once assaulted publicly by Sir Wm. Phipps—until 1707, when John Jekyll, Esq., nephew of the celebrated Sir Joseph Jekyll, obtained the collectorship and held it until his death, Dec. 30, 1731. He was an honest and upright man. His son John, who married the beautiful Miss Margaret Shippe of Philadelphia, succeeded him, and remained in office until his decease, March 1st, 1741,[1] when John Peagrum,

[1] Collectors prior to the revolution.

Edward Randolph.,	1681—1690.
William Brenton, Esq.,	1691—1707.
John Jekyll, Esq.,	1707—1731.
John Jekyll [son of the preceding].,	1731—1740.
Sir Charles Henry Frankland,	1741—1757.
Benjamin Parsons, Esq.,	1757—1759.
George Cradock, Esq.,	1759—1763.
Roger Hale, Esq.,	1763—
Joseph Harrison, Esq.,	1768—1775.

Esq., surveyor general of his majesty's customs for the northern district of North America, appointed William Sheaffe,[1] Esq., as collector, pro tempore.

Although the royal governors and other officers of the crown had been incessantly engaged in altercations with the general court and people, who were becoming more and more jealous of their inalienable rights, — more and more restive under the dictation of the favorites of Bolingbroke, Walpole, and Newcastle, still, from the times of Brenton down to the opening scenes of the revolution, the collectors of the customs appear to have performed their official duties with general acceptance, and to have escaped in a remarkable degree the odium which fell upon the heads of the other colonial functionaries of the English government. It is more than probable that they often favored the American traders by a liberal interpretation[2] of the regulations of the board of trade; and it is certain that they were gentlemen of good sense and breeding, and that they identified themselves, to some extent, with the general interests and prosperity of the people. The Jekylls were highly esteemed and popular citizens; and when Charles Henry Frankland entered on the duties of his office in the autumn of 1741, I cannot discover that any special prejudice or cause of complaint existed against the revenue system, or the manner in which it was conducted;

[1] Deputy collector, 1741 – 1768.

[2] "The officers of the customsused to permit evasions of the law as the only means of acquiring wealth."—Bancroft's *Hist. United States America*, vol. IV, p. 339.

nor did any strong opposition manifest itself until the accession of George the Third, the consequent elevation of the Earl of Bute, who insisted on taxing America, and the granting of the celebrated writs of assistance, to the officers of the customs to enable them to enforce the iniquitous acts of trade.

CHAPER IV.

Salary of Frankland — Official order — King's chapel — Visit to Marblehead — Agnes Surriage — Her poverty — Employment — Beauty — Removal to Boston — Amusements of Frankland — Gifts to Harvard College — Official records.

The nominal salary of Frankland as collector was but £100 sterling,[1] and yet the perquisites of his office were such as to afford him a large income. His name first appears in connection with his official business in an order in the *Evening Post*, dated Dec. 2d, 1741, to the effect that "coasters must not fail to be entered and cleared at the Custom house[2] as the statute demands." He became at once an attendant on the ministry of the Rev. Roger Price, at the King's chapel, which, having been built of wood in 1689, was already falling to decay, — and he con-

[1] "1748. Sir Henry Frankland, collector, Boston, salary £100. Wm. Lambert, surveyor, salary £70. — See *Present State of Great Britain.*

[2] The office of Edward Randolph was on the corner of Richmond and North street, and was standing until within a few years. When George Cradock, Esq., was appointed collector, the Custom house was removed to the house of John Wendell, Esq. *See Gen. Reg.*, Jan. 1854, p. 28. At the time of the massacre, which occured in front of it, March 5, 1770, the Custom house was on the lower corner of Royal Exchange lane, now Exchange street, and King, now State street. Sometime after the revolution, the commodious building was erected on Custom-house street, and the trade of Boston rapidly increasing, the present noble structure of granite, in the form of a Greek cross, was erected at an expense of about $1,076,000, and was opened Aug. 1, 1847.

tributed, near the close of 1741, the sum of £50[1] sterling towards the erection of the present noble edifice.

In the summer of 1742, the town of Marblehead[2] was authorized to erect a fortification, since called Fort Sewall,[3] for the defence of its harbor against the French cruisers, and £690 were appropriated for this object by the government. On a visit to this place, undertaken it might have been with the view of promoting this work, or of transacting business pertaining to the revenues — for this flourishing town had already become a port of entry — Frankland's attention was arrested by a very beautiful girl,[4] some sixteen summers old, who happened at the time to be engaged in the very ungraceful occupation of scrubbing the floor of the tavern where he stopped. Her dress was poor and scanty, and her feet were destitute of shoes and stockings.

---

1 The principal contributors were Mr. Faneuil, £200 sterling (that is £2000 old tenor); Mr. Shirley £100, sterling, and Sir Henry Frankland £50 sterling. *Hist. of King's Chapel*, p. 111.

2 Marmaracria opidum maritum, saxis abundans, inde novanglicè dictum, MARBLEHEAD, asperima vox aures Latinas horride per stringens. — *Prof. Stephen Sewall.*

This town has been denominated elsewhere, from its rocks, "marmoreum promontorium." When Whitfield visited the town, he said, pointing to the rocks, — Pray where do they bury their dead?

3 Ceded to the U. S. in 1794, and rebuilt on a larger scale in 1863.

4 The account of this visit to Marblehead and interview with Agnes and the Surriage family is from Mrs. Swain by Mrs. Hildreth: from Isaac Surriage by Mrs. Dawes and others.

She was a "waiting girl of all work" at the village inn—it might have been the Fountain House,[1] near the fort—and her wretched garb at once declared that she was of the humbler class of waiting girls. But though so meanly clad and servilely employed, the young collector instantly discovered in her form and features gleams of sparkling beauty. Her ringlets were as black and glossy as the raven; her dark eyes beamed with light and loveliness; her voice was musical, birdlike; and she bore the charming name of Agnes Surriage.[2] Frankland called her from her scrubbing kindly to him, made some inquiries in relation to her parents,[3] and perceiving that her wit was equal to her beauty, gave her a crown to buy a pair of shoes, and then bore home with him, as we may well suppose, the image of this beautiful waiting-maid of Marblehead.

Visiting the town sometime afterwards, perhaps in the autumn of the same year, he was surprised

---

[1] There used to be a large building occupied as a tavern by Mary Dolliver in Fountain Garden in colonial times.—*Town Records*.

[2] Noble, in his *Memoirs of the House of Cromwell*, erroneously calls her Agnes Browne.

[3] I find on examining the records of the 2d church in Marblehead, that "Edward Surriage owned the covenant, May 15th, 1720," and that "Mary, wife of Edward Surriage, was admitted to full communion, Aug. 27th, 1727." Their son, Edward, was baptized July 5, 1719; Mary in 1722; Josiah in 1724; AGNES, April 17, 1726; Thomas, May 5, 1728; John, June 28, 1730; Hugh, in Sept., 1732; Isaac, a son still younger, m. Ruhamah Pedrick, Sept. 5, 1768. She was admitted to full communion, April 29, 1770, and their daughter, Jane, afterwards Mrs. Pelatiah Bixby, was baptized at Marblehead in January, 1774.

to find Agnes Surriage working still without shoes and stockings, and to his enquiry why she had not purchased them, she replied with charming naiveté: "I have indeed, sir, with the crown you gave me; but I keep them to wear to meeting." The elegance of her lithe and slender form, the sprightliness of her mind, the artlessness and modesty of her ways, quite entranced the heart of Frankland, and he sought, and gained permission of her parents, Edward and Mary Surriage, who were then poor, but pious people, to remove her to Boston to be educated. On coming to town, Agnes was immediately permitted to enjoy the best educational advantages which the place then afforded. She was taught reading, writing, grammar, music, dancing, embroidery, and whatever graces and accomplishments were thought requisite to form a fashionable and perfect lady. In acquiring a polite education she did not, however, lose the artless simplicity of her childhood, nor the pious counsel of her mother and the Rev. Dr. Edward Holyoke,[1] her pastor at Marblehead. Thus several summers passed away, Frankland attending to the duties of his office, talking politics, with John. Overing,[2] Charles Apthorp, or

[1] Born in Boston 1689, ordained at Marblehead, April, 25th, 1716, where he continued until 1737, when he was chosen president of Harvard College. He died June 1, 1769.

[2] Allied to the noble family of Lord St. John Bolingbroke; came to Boston in 1720 and lived in School street. He m. Henrietta, daughter of Judge Robert Auchmuty, by whom he had an only daughter Elizabeth who was married to Dr. John Wilson of Hopkinton, in 1750. He was a remarkably fluent and agreeable speaker, and was appointed attorney general in 1733, which office he held at the time of his death in 1748.

Robert Auchmuty, reading the *Gentleman's Magazine*, the *Spectator*, or the *Boston Evening Post*,— driving out to Cambridge, Salem, or Marblehead; or playing whist and dominoes with Gov. Shirley and his accomplished lady Frances, while Agnes Surriage was steadily pursuing her studies under Peter Pelham,[1] or other instructors of that day. Among the scanty records of Frankland's life at this period, I find that he gave a "ring dial and a spirit level"[2] to Harvard College in 1743, and I have discovered the two following brief documents, bearing his large, bold signature, filed away among the state papers of Massachusetts.

"These certify that bond is here given relating to the register of the sloop Sea Flower, Benjamin Holt, pursuant to act of parliament. Dated Custom House, Boston, 30th March, 1743. H. FRANKLAND, Coll."

"Port of Boston. These certify that security is here given relating to the registry of the sloop Enterprise, Richard Waite, master, at present lost, or mislaid, pursuant to act of parliament. Dated at the Custom House, the 28th of April, 1743. H. FRANKLAND, Coll."

"Sloop Enterprise, Richard Waite, square sterned, fifty-five tons, built at Newbury, 1741, by Thos. Perkins.

---

[1] He was teaching school in Leverett lane, near King street, 1741.

[2] See Quincy's *Hist. of Harvard College*, vol. II, p. 531. App. He also gave to the college in 1757, a small electrical apparatus and a number of books;—also, at another time, several books. Id. pp. 528, 531.

CHAPTER V.

Captain Thomas Frankland — Visit to Boston — Address to him — Subscriptions at King's Chapel — Reduction of Louisbourg — Diversions of the Collector.

In the summer of 1743, the Rose frigate,[1] 20 guns, entered the harbor of Boston, and its popular commander, Captain Thomas Frankland, eldest brother of the collector, was most cordially received by the people. He was appointed to the command of this noted vessel, July 15, 1740, and at the close of that year conveyed Gov. Tinker to the Bahama Islands and for some time cruised in that region, for the protection of the coast against the Spaniards. In June, 1742, after a gallant action of two hours, he captured a Spanish vessel of 20 guns, with two armed prizes; and on the last day of the year he took a large Bermuda sloop and a Dutch snow, with a vast amount of silver. The next year he was married to Miss Sarah, daughter of Judge Rhett of South Carolina, a very beautiful and accomplished lady, then eighteen years of age; and on his arrival in Boston to visit his brother, the following complimentary lines were addressed to him, in the *Evening Post*, of the 22d of August.

---

[1] This Frigate commanded by Captain George, visited Boston as early as 1686, bringing the Rev. Robert Ratcliffe, the first Episcopal minister of Boston. See *Hist. of King's Chapel*, p. 13.

TO CAPTAIN FRANKLAND, COMMANDER OF HIS MAJESTY'S SHIP ROSE, NOW IN BOSTON.

From peaceful solitude and calm retreat,
I now and then look out upon the great;
Praise where 'tis due I'll give; no servile tool
Of honorable knave, or reverend fool:
Surplice, or red coat, both alike to me:
Let him that wears them great and worthy be,
Whether a coward in the camp, or port,
Traitor in want, or traitor in the court,
Alike reward their cowardice deserves;
Alike their treachery, he who eats or starves,
Or brave by land, or hero on the main,
Alike respect their courage should sustain.
Then let me lisp thy name, thy praise rehearse,
Though in weak numbers and in feeble verse.
Though faint the whisper when the thunder roars,
And speak thee great through all Hispania's shores,
Still safe in port the red coat chief may scare,
Dread of the boys and favorite of the fair,
Still shudder at the dangers of the deep;
To arms an enemy; but a friend to sleep.
We see thee, FRANKLAND, dreadful o'er the main,
Not terrible to children, but to Spain.
With thee, thy dawning beams of glory play,
And triumph in the prospect of the day.
O, let the kindling spark, the glowing fire
Your generous soul inflame as once your Sire;[1]
With him the schemes of tyranny oppose,
And love your country as you hate her foes.

After spending some time in delightful intercourse with his brother; enjoying the hospitalities, and visiting the environs of Boston, which were, then, mostly an unbroken forest; after interchanging pleasant words with the beautiful Agnes Surriage, now fresh with the bloom of seventeen sum-

[1] Oliver Cromwell, Lord Protector.

mers, the gallant commander of the Rose frigate, sailed away to gain brighter laurels by his conquests on the main; while the collector remained busily employed in taking care of the revenues, in discussing the questions now coming to an open issue between France and England; or spending once in a while, by way of amusement, a day in the chase, of which he was a hearty lover; or in a pleasant excursion in the custom house boat to Nahant or Marblehead. But few traces of his life at this period, however, remain to gratify our curiosity. In the treasurer's account with King's Chapel I find, under date of Oct. 9, 1744, an acknowledgement of "ten pounds by Henry Frankland, Esq., to Easter last," and under date of Aug. 6, 1745, appears the following entry: "By Henry Frankland, Esq., for last year's deficiency to Easter, £10."

This year is rendered memorable by the opening of what is called King George's war, involving the possessions of France and England in America, and by the brilliant expedition of Gov. Wm. Shirley to Louisbourg and the reduction of that strong hold[1] of the French in this country. Massachusetts furnished about 3000 men for this enterprise, so that Boston in the early part of the season was alive with military bustle and excitement.[2] The position of Frankland as collector, prevented him from taking any very prominent part in the war,

[1] The fortress surrendered to the combined forces of Commodore Peter Warren and Sir William Pepperrell, June 28, 1745.

[2] Drake's *History of Boston*, p. 620.

and we hear of him only as making one or two patriotic addresses to the citizens of Boston just previous to the embarkation of the troops for Louisbourg.

He must have shared in the public rejoicings at the reception of the news on the 2d of July of the success of Shirley, when the town was "universally illuminated," but while the governor was winning those laurels in the field which render his name illustrious; the courtly officer of the customs was doubtless endeavouring to prevent the smuggling of rum and sugars into port, or talking politics at the Royal Exchange Tavern,[1] hunting foxes with Commissary Price, or entertaining the high bred dames at the north end with anecdotes of Robert Walpole, Henry Pelham, or King George the Second.

---

[1] This was in King, now State street, and is noticed as early as 1727.

CHAPTER VI.

Purchase of land at Pemaquid — The Brown Rights — Description of the land — Various claimants.

At the close of the year 1745, Frankland purchased of the mother of Agnes, for the sum of £50 lawful money, her right and title to one seventh part of a vast tract of land in Maine, which had fallen to her on the decease of her father, Richard Pierce, of New Harbor. Mrs. Surriage was then a widow; she was poor, but she was descended from the celebrated John Brown, who settled at Pemaquid, now Bristol, but a few years after the landing of the Pilgrims at Plymouth, and who purchased of the two Indian sagamores, Captain John Samoset and Unnongoit, July 15, 1625, that territory in Lincoln county, Me., known as the Brown Right, respecting which there has been such long and bitter controversies. It appears that Richard Pierce married a daughter of John Brown, and purchased land of the Indians, about eight miles above his father-in-law's plantation, at New Harbor, living thereon until the time of King Phillip's war, when John Pierce,[1] a brother of Mrs. Surriage,

[1] "When the wars with the Indians broke out, I, the deponent, took a vessel and 30 men, and brought my father's family away from thence, [that is from Miscongus]. John Pierce. Nov. 20, 1764." *See Report of Commissioners to Gen. Court of Massachusetts, on Lincoln County Difficulties, May,* 1811.

obtained a vessel, and removed the whole family to Marblehead. The fort at Pemaquid was destroyed by the Indians in 1696, and the plantations so broken up that the land had become of very little value, yet the number of claimants to a title in it was continually increasing. The paper conveying Mrs. Surriage's right in this property to Frankland, I have found among the Suffolk county deeds. It bears date Dec. 19, 1745, and describes the estate as follows: "A tract of Maine lands and islands, lying and being at a place called Miscongus, in that part of New England that lyes between Kennebeck River and River St. Croix,—said tract extending from Pemaquid Falls eastward and northward as far as the utmost limits contained in the original Sachem's deeds of said lands, made to my grand-father, John Brown,[1] and father, Richard Pierce, both deceased, which lye at Somerset Cove, Broad Bay, Round Pond, New Harbour, or any other place or places whatever, comprehended within the limits of the aforesaid deeds, being one seventh part of all said tract, as described and bounded therein, as of right descended to me as

[1] He lived at New Harbor where he died, leaving a widow who remarried. One of his sons, John B. Brown, removed to Framingham, Mass. He conveyed his lands at New Harbor to his only son John of Saco, Dec. 7, 1720. In the original Indian deed this Brown tract is described as beginning at Pemaquid Falls and so running a direct course to the head of New Harbor, from thence, to the south end of Muscongus Island, taking in the Island and so running five and twenty miles into the country north and east, and thence eight miles northwest and by west, and then turning and running south and by west to Pemaquid. The consideration was 50 skins!"

one of the heirs at law to the said John Brown and Richard Pierce." Signed in presence of Peter Brazier and Nath'l Bethune, Boston. The original deed having been burned in the court house at Boston a few years later, and the patent of John Pierce, who was associated with Brown in the original settlement, being lost—it was found after awhile that several claims covered the same territory, and thus the "rights and titles" became more and more involved and complicated, until settled by an act of legislature in 1811.[1]

Mrs. Surriage was doubtless entitled to a seventh part of her father's estate; but whether Frankland ever realized any thing from his purchase, I have not been able to determine. He probably bought the land for the sake of aiding gracefully the widowed mother of his favorite ward.

[1] The four principal *claims* were the Brown, the Drowne, the Tappan, and the Lincoln academy *rights*. The Brown claim covers most of the town of Bristol, all of Nobleborough and Jefferson, and a part of Newcastle. The Drowne and Tappan claims embrace nearly the same land. The Drowne right is founded on a patent from the King of England to Robert Alsworth and Gyles Elbridge of Bristol, Eng., dated Feb. 20, 1631, that is, nearly six years after the date of the Brown deed from the Indians, who were the owners in fee simple of the territory. Richard Pierce, the father of Mrs. Edward Surriage, lived at Miscongus; but afterwards bought land of the Indians about 8 miles above his father-in-law's plantation at New Harbor, on which he settled and lived in a garrison house. Her brother John, a baker, who brought the family away from the perils of that early settlement, was living at Marblehead in 1764, then over 70 years of age. The following proprietors of Pemaquid, met at the Orange Tree Tavern, Boston, Aug. 31, 1743. "Habijah Savage, Joshua Winslow, Jonas Clarke, Thomas Rusk, Joseph Fitch and Shem Drowne." Pemaquid Point

CHAPTER VII.

Visit of Admiral Peter Warren and Gen. William Pepperrell to Boston — Rev. Roger Price — Rev. Henry Caner — Subscription of Frankland to King's Chapel — He succeeds to the Baronetcy of Thirsk — His relation to Agnes Surriage — State of feeling in Boston.

The summer of 1746, Frankland spent in performing the duties pertaining to his office, and in the enjoyment of the festivity of that gay season. The heroes of Louisbourg, Admiral Peter Warren[1] and Gen. Wm. Pepperrell, arrived at Boston in the Chester, 50 guns — with a blue flag at her mizzen topmast — on the 24th of June, and were most cordially welcomed by the people. Military parades, public receptions, private parties, balls, and excursions to Lynn in Captain Alley's new packet; to Salem, Marblehead and the college at Cambridge; to Roxbury, Dedham, and even as far as Hopkinton, evinced the gratitude of the people to their distinguished visitors; and in these rejoicings Frankland — who was an intimate friend of Admiral

---

is one of the most beautiful headlands on our coast; its early history abounds in romantic details of conflicts with the French and Indians, and John Brown, its original proprietor, may be justly styled the father of the state of Maine.

[1] Sir Peter Warren, Admiral of the Blue, and called the naval hero of Louisbourg, was born in Ireland, 1703, was made Captain in 1727, and commanded the "Squirrel," 40 guns, against Carthagena, 1740. He was made Knight of the Order of Bath in 1748. He married Susanna, daughter of Stephen De Lancey and Ann Van Cortlandt, of New York.

Warren, — and Agnes Surriage must have taken a very lively and conspicuous part. In the difficulties, too, between the imperious rector, Roger Price, and the King's Chapel, which led to his resignation on Thanksgiving day, of the same year, the courtly collector was deeply concerned. The loss of his clerical companion did not, however, at all abate his interest in the prosperity of the church, for on Thursday following the induction of the Rev. Henry Caner[1] into office, the Records inform us that "Henry Frankland, Esq., bought pew No. 6 in the old house, for £30," and the yearly contributions of that pew were very liberal,[2] until the removal of the house. In August of the same year he stood as sponsor with Henry Caswell and Mary Gooch for Henry, son of Samuel and Elizabeth Wentworth; and at a meeting held at the Rev. Mr. Caner's house, at which were present, Governor William Shirley, Eliakim Hutchinson,[3] Charles Apthorp, and others, he gave £150 sterling,[4] on the new subscription for the rebuilding

[1] The Rev. Dr. Henry Caner, b. 1707, graduated at Yale college, 1724, was inducted into his office as Rector of King's Chapel, by Commissary Price, on the 11th of April, 1747. He was from the church in Fairfield, Connecticut, and left Boston for Halifax, 1776. He d. 1792. — Sprague's *Annals of Am. Pulpit*, vol. V.

[2] This pew contributed in 1748, £16 15*s*. 10*d*.; in 1749, £18 7*s*. 4*d*.; in 1750, £14 8*s*. 1*d*,; 1751, £9; in 1752, £10 4*s*. 1*d*.; in 1753, £7 15*s*. 9*d*.; and in 1754, £132 0*s*. 6*d*.

[3] Warden of King's Chapel, 1743. He m. Elizabeth, daughter of Gov. Shirley, and owned an estate in Walpole, which was confiscated in 1776, and thence occupied by my grandfather, Thomas, and his two brothers, Nathaniel and Willoughby Nason.

[4] See *Hist. King's Chapel*, page 112.

of the chapel. By the death of his uncle, Sir Thomas Frankland, M. P., and one of the Lords of the Admiralty, this summer, the baronetcy of Thirsk now devolved on him, as the nearest blood relative, and he received the title of SIR CHARLES HENRY FRANKLAND, Bart.[1]

Agnes Surriage was now coming into the opening bloom of womanhood, and was living in the family of the accomplished baronet. She was radiant in beauty; of refined and gentle manners; but of ignoble birth; she had won unconsciously, her benefactor's heart; yet it would seem an unpardonable indignity to his proud race to bestow on her his hand. He took advantage of his high position, and with many a graceful word and winning smile, succeeded at length in gaining the entire ascendency over her affections. A few aged persons in Boston can well remember hearing their grand parents speak of the indignant feelings of the school companions[2] of Agnes Surriage, when it was publicly known that an improper intimacy existed between her and the baronet; and although

---

[1] The business of the custom house at this period may be inferred from the following statement:

From Christmas 1747, to Christmas 1748, 500 vessels cleared out of this port [Boston], only for a foreign trade, and 430 were entered inwards, to say nothing of coasting and fishing vessels, both of which are extremely numerous, and said to be equal in number to the others.—Burke's *Settlements in America*, p. 329.

1749. Entries at the port of Boston, 489. Clearances, 504. See Holmes's *Annals*.

[2] From Mrs. Dawes, Mrs. Hildreth and others;—one of these school companions was afterwards Mrs. Boardman, of Boston.

the morality of Boston had at that time been greatly vitiated by the officials of the crown, such was the stern integrity of the people still, that a storm of just indignation rose against an alliance unsanctioned by the holy rite of matrimony, which neither wealth, nor noble name, nor official power, nor courtly manners, could allay; and therefore, the young collector resolved to seek a residence for himself, Agnes and his retainers, in the seclusion of the country.

CHAPTER VIII.

Frankland purchases land at Magunco in Hopkinton — Description of the place — He erects a mansion — His life at Hopkinton — Convivial habits — Custom House papers — Attorney to the widow of Sir Peter Warren.

The Rev. Roger Price[1] had already taken up an extensive tract of land in Hopkinton,[2] one of the

[1] Roger Price, Commissary of the Bishop of London, was appointed rector of King's Chapel in 1729, in which office he continued until Nov. 1746, when he read his letter of resignation, and in the ensuing summer sailed for England in the Mermaid man-of-war. He returned soon after and remained in this country until the summer of 1753. He married Elizabeth, daughter of John Bull, by whom he had I, Elizabeth b. 1734, resided in Hopkinton, was strong minded and charitable, and died in Boston, July 3, 1826; II, William, a major in the British army, who d. at Hopkinton, Dec. 7, 1802, leaving two natural daughters, Mary, who m. Lawson Valentine, Dec. 15, 1817, and Olivia, who m. Benjamin H. Hall, July, 28, 1818; III, Henry Yelverton, who d. Aug. 14, 1780, aged 39; IV, Thomas, who was drowned while skating, in the Serpentine river, and V, Andrew, who was a clergyman, and d. June 7, 1851. Roger Price went to Hopkinton about the year 1743 and purchased a tract of 709 acres of land "on the banks of a noble river," to which 142 acres of common land were added in 1745. He soon after, about 1750, erected a church and endowed it with a glebe of 170 acres, the deed of which is dated July 9, 1748.

[2] This town, incorporated in 1715, lies about 25 miles south west of Boston. It received its name from Edward Hopkins, Esq., whose liberal bequest of £500 to Harvard College was laid out in the purchase of land which together with land granted by the general court forms the town.

most romantic towns in Middlesex county, and had resolved to build a mission church for the accommodation of such Episcopalians as had, or might, become residents in the place. This circumstance, together with the excellent quality of the soil and the beauty of the scenery, induced Frankland to select this town for his retirement from the annoyance of the busy tongues of Boston. He accordingly made a purchase of 482 acres of land, in 1751 and 2, in the easterly part of this newly settled town for a plantation. The tract was purchased from several individuals,[1] and lies along the southern

---

He preached here about three years and was an intimate friend of Sir Chas. Henry Frankland. He d. at Leigh, England, Dec. 8, 1762. See Sprague's *Annals of American Pulpit*, vol. V, in loco; also Rev. Nathaniel Howe's *Century Sermon*, p, 31.—The present Episcopal church was erected in 1818. The Bible and Prayer Book were presented by Madam Elizabeth Price.

The town discounted the following churchmen's rates in 1752. Sir Henry Frankland, Thomas Higgins, Julius Chase, each £1, 1*s.* 1*d.* 1*qr.* William Wesson, 7*s.* 9*d.* Captain David Ellis, 10*s.* 3*d.* John Devine, 4*s.* 8*d.* Thomas Valentine, 5*s.* 1*d.* Patrick White, 5*s.* 10*d.* 2*qr.* John Mastick, 3*s.* 3*d.* 3*qr.* Robert Barrett, 6*s.* 9*d.* 1*qr.* James Fanning, 2*s.* 8*d.* Thomas Chaddock, 5*s.* 11*d*, 2*qr.* William Browne, 6*s.* 0*d* 2*qr.* Patrick Shay [father of Daniel Shay, the rebel,] 4*s.* 1*d.* Hugh Demsey, 2*s.* Richard Kelly 5*s.* 7*d.* 3*qr.* Rebecca Wilson, 2*s.* 9*d.* 3*qr.* Peter Vialas, 5*s.* 6*d.* 3*qr.* Jno. Kelly, 3*s.* 10*d.* 1*qr.* Mrs. Dench, 2*s.* 8*d.* 3*qr.*—*Town Records.*

[1] Dec 22, 1750. Laid out to Henry Frankland, and his heirs forever, 48½ acres of land in Hopkinton in full of his right, and Jacob Parker's right (in the 2d division), being 321 acres, with allowance for highways, as is bounded and described by the plan annexed. January 7, 1750–51, this plan was accepted by the proprietors.—*Town Records.*

1751, Dec. 20. Benjamin Barnard of Framingham, sold Sir Henry Frankland 13 acres of land for £100, old tenor.—*Id.*

and western slope of a noble eminence, called in the Nipmuck tongue, Magunco,[1] or the place of great trees, where the celebrated John Eliot had in earlier times an Indian church. The summit of the hill now covered with a fine growth of thrifty chestnut commands a view of the peaks of the Wachusett and Monadnock mountains on the north west, of the beautiful village of Hopkinton and Hayden Row on the south west; of a rich and varied landscape on the south, and of the charming village of Ashland,[2] in the valley where the Concord river and the Cold Springs[3] blend their waters in

---

[1] One of the veteran chestnut trees of Magunco, still remaining on the left hand side of the road as you approach the Frankland House, is 21 feet in circumference; and our earnest word for it is, "*Woodman, spare that tree.*"

Of this place General Daniel Gookin writes in 1774:—"The number of their families is about 11 and about 55 souls. The Indians plant upon a great hill which is very fertile. Their ruler's name is Pamhaman, a sober, active man and pious; their teacher's name is Job, a person well accepted for piety and abilities among them. They have plenty of corn and keep some cattle, horses, and swine, for which the place is well accommodated." See *Mass. Hist. Coll.* vol. I.—The tract of land occupied by the praying Indians, and called Magunco, embraced according to an old chart 1152 acres, and was purchased of the Indians, 1710 or 11. It is now mostly within the town of Ashland. The plateau on which the village of Ashland stands was granted to the celebrated Col. Wm. Crowne, Oct. 8, 1662. It was conveyed to Savill Simpson of Boston, cordwainer, for £30, and afterwards came into possession of Col. John Jones, who m. Hannah, daughter of Savill Simpson.—See *Hist. of Framingham*, by Rev. Wm. Barry, p. 9.

[2] Set off, in part, from H. in 1846 - It embraces the Frankland place.

[3] So called from the numerous cold springs, teeming with trout, which form the stream. The name is in Col. Crowne's grant, 1662.

the east. The hill side to the south and west abounds in cool and gushing springlets which leaving lines of freshest verdure in their course, unite and form a brook, well stored with trout, and large enough to turn a mill; and which sweeping round the south eastern base of Magunco, passes through a pleasant valley into the Cold Spring stream.

On an eligible and commanding site upon the southwestern inclination of this Indian hill, the baronet erected a commodious manor house in 1751; reduced about 130 acres of his land to tillage, planted an extensive orchard, built a costly barn,[1] 100 feet in length and surmounted by a cupola; a granary which was set upon elaborately wrought freestone pillars; and houses for his servants equal to those of many of the farmers in the neighborhood. Having a taste for horticulture, he introduced a great variety of the choicest fruit,— such as apples, pears, plums, peaches, cherries of excellent quality, apricots and quinces from England:—and having an eye for beauty, he set out elms and other ornamental trees upon his grounds, and embellished his walks and garden with the box,[2] the lilac, hawthorn and the rose: some portion of this shrubbery still blooms as beautifully as when King George the Second sat upon the throne.

The mansion was large and strongly built. It stood at some distance from the main road, and was

[1] Blown down in the terrific gale, Sept. 23, 1815.

[2] Two rows of box still remain, having attained the height of about ten feet; it is the largest [1862] in the country. The trunks of some of the lilacs are eight inches in diameter, and the red roses still continue to bloom as in times of old.

approached by a noble avenue cut through the chestnut forest, and by a flower garden tastefully arranged in front. The spacious hall, sustained by fluted columns, was hung with tapestry, richly ornamented with dark figures on a ground of deepest green, according to the fashion of the times. The chimney pieces were of Italian marble; and cornices of stucco-work and other costly finishing embellished the parlor, anterooms and chambers.

The grounds immediately around the house were formed into terraces, by the hands of slaves, and the waters from the living springs[1] above, clothed them in liveliest verdure.

To this beautiful retreat Frankland retired in the summer of 1752, with Agnes Surriage and a natural son, named Henry Cromwell, then about twelve years of age. Here, it seems, from tradition, and from what I have been able to glean from the records of those days, they spent the time in directing the affairs of the plantation, upon which not less than a dozen slaves[2] were employed; in deer[3] and fox hunting; in angling for the speckled trout in Cold Spring brook—in reading the works of Richardson, Steele, Swift, Addison and

[1]No less than five springs flow from the southern side of Magunco.

[2]The whole number of slaves in Hopkinton in 1754, above the age of 16, was 15; in the state, about 4580.—See *Mass. Hist. Coll.* Vol. III, p. 95, second series.—Jackee, a negro, and Cato, a negro, were received into the Rev. Mr. Barrett's church in 1741. —*Church Records.*

[3]Two men were chosen annually by the town, at that period, as deer reeves.—*Town Records.*

Pope; in cultivating flowers and music, of which Agnes was passionately fond; in entertaining the Wilsons, Valentines,[1] and Joneses, of Hopkinton; the Auchmutys, Brinleys, Overings and Stoddards of Boston; in those various sports, pleasures, pastimes and festivities, for which the house of a wealthy English baronet of that period was celebrated.

The form of religion was, indeed, observed; the prayer book was read; the sermon of Rev. Roger Price in his new church upon the rocks of Hopkinton, or of Rev. Henry Caner of King's Chapel, was duly heard; but the spirit of religion was most lamentably wanting.

As collector of the port of Boston, Frankland made the acquaintance of the costliest wines which Europe could afford, and his ample and well constructed wine cellar was always stored with the very choicest brands. In his festivities he is said to have used himself a winecup[2] made of double thickness, and thus containing but half as much as those of his boon companions, who, being constrained to drink as many bumpers as himself, soon lost their senses, while he continued sober.

While Frankland was thus engaged in the pleasures of country life at Hopkinton, it does not

---

[1] The Valentine place is upon the eastern slope of Magunco, and adjoins the Frankland place.

[2] One of his winecups is still in the possession of Mrs. Mary Ann Bigelow, daughter of Dr. John Overing Wilson. The bowl is very small and stands upon a long slender stem, which has a crimson-tinted spiral line running through the centre.

appear that he was inattentive to his duties as collector. In the *Boston Gazette*, Feb. 27, 1753, he published under his own signature the following notice, which reveals his faithfulness in collecting the revenues, as well as some of the trials to which he was subjected by the smugglers of that period.

"Boston, Feb. 19th, 1753.—Whereas, I am informed there still continues to be carried on an illicit trade between Holland and other parts of Europe, and the neighboring colonies; and that great quantities of European and Asiatic commodities are clandestinely brought from thence into this port by land as well as by sea, and as I am determined to use my utmost endeavors to prevent the carrying on of a trade so prejudicial to our mother country and detrimental to the fair trader. I hereby again give this public notice that, if any person or persons will give me information where such goods are concealed, that they may be proceeded against according to law, they, upon condemnation, shall be very handsomely rewarded, and their names concealed; and I hereby direct all the officers of the customs within my district to be very vigilant in discovering and seizing all such contraband goods.

"H. Frankland, Coll."

Mar. 12. From the records of Hopkinton, it appears that the town voted to grant Sir Henry Frankland's request, in respect to a road through the land that
" 20. was Jeremiah Hobbs's, and "that £1 8*s*. 1*d*., were discounted from his rates, by reason of his being a churchman." I find, also, that he was appointed

about this time an attorney to the widow of his friend, Sir Peter Warren, who had died in England the preceding year. It is thus recorded in the registry of deeds, for Suffolk county: "Sir Henry Frankland, Bart., Charles Apthorp,[1] and Thomas Hancock, were appointed attorneys' to Lady Susanna Warren, widow of Sir Peter Warren of London." May 16.

[1]One of the greatest merchants of his time, who d. in 1758, aged 61, leaving about £50,000.

CHAPTER IX.

Frankland visits England — Cold reception of Agnes Surriage — Law suit with his mother — Makes the tour of Europe — Comes to reside at Lisbon — State of society there — Frankland's philosophy.

It became necessary the ensuing year, 1754, that
Frankland should visit England, and the last record of him, previous to his departure, is an ac-
knowledgment of a contribution of £45 sterling,
April 23. for King's Chapel, which was now nearly completed,
and which was opened by a sermon by Rev. Henry
" 21. Caner, the following August. He was called home
to carry on a suit at law, in which the will of the
late Sir Thomas Frankland, bequeathing his whole
estate at Thirkelby to his lady, was contested.
Leaving therefore, the custom house in charge of
Mr. William Sheaffe, as deputy collector, he em-
barked with Agnes Surriage for London, where he
arrived early in the summer, and attempted to
introduce her into the circle of his distinguished
relatives, one of whom had just married Thomas
May 15. Pelham, 1st Earl of Chichester. In spite, however,
of his solicitations on her behalf, his fair ward was
treated with justly deserved disdain by his proud
family, and the trials and mortifications to which
she was then subjected were among the most painful experiences of her eventful life. She keenly
felt the ignominy of her false position; nor could

the assiduous attention of her soi-disant protector alleviate her misery. Her mother's humble cottage among the rocks of Marblehead would have been far more pleasant than the costly halls of the Franklands, where cold civilities informed her constantly that she was an unwelcome guest.

An account of the suit at law and trial is given in the *Gentleman's Magazine*, as follows: June 4.

"A cause between Sir Harry Frankland, plaintiff, and the Lady of the late Sir Thomas, defendant, was tried in the court of the King's Bench, by a special jury. The subject of litigation was a will of Sir Thomas, suspected to be made when he was not of sound mind, and it appeared that he had made three;—one in 1741, another in 1744, and a third in 1746. In the first, only a slender provision was made for his Lady; by the second, this family estate in Yorkshire, of £2,500 per annum, was given her for life; and by the third, the whole estate, both real and personal, was left to be disposed of at her discretion, without any provision for the heirs at law. The jury, after having withdrawn for about an hour and a half, set aside the last, and confirmed the second. In a hearing before the Lord Chancellor, some time afterwards, in relation to the costs of the suit, it was decreed that the Lady should pay them all, both at common law July. and in chancery."

Having settled his affairs in England, the barronet made, in company with his fair protégé, the customary tour of Europe, and came at the close of this, or the beginning of the next year, to reside,

either for the sake of health, or for the transaction of some business for the English government, at Lisbon, in the kingdom of Portugal. This country had been for many years in alliance with Great Britain, and was now under King Joseph the First, reaping rich harvests of gold from its Brazilian possessions in America. Lisbon, the capital, was increasing rapidly in wealth and splendor, and had already become a kind of commercial rendezvous for the English merchants. They had established a large factory here, and the city was teeming with Englishmen who had come hither for the purposes of trade, or health, or pleasure. Dr. Philip Doddridge had closed his valuable life here, in 1751; Maj. Frederick Frankland, a near relative of Sir
July 15. Charles, died here in 1752; the eloquent George
Whitfield visited the city in 1754, and Henry Field-
1754. ing, the great English novelist, breathed his last in
Oct. 8. this voluptuous capital, which he admirably describes, a little prior to the arrival of the party whose singular and eventful course I am attempting to delineate. Lisbon was at this period full of life and gaiety; money was abundant; public entertainments and receptions of the great were frequent and splendid; and the opera was said to be the finest in Europe. The young king and his court were popular with the people, and the pomp and ceremony at the papal hierarchy was never more imposing. To this sensuous and dissolute city, Sir Charles Henry Frankland introduced the beautiful Agnes and entered—not, however, without some misgivings, upon the gay round of fashionable life.

He hired and furnished a house; adopted, as his means now warranted, a courtly style of living, and although a communicant of the church of England, allowed himself to be guided more and more by the light, superficial and convenient philosophy of Montaigne, Rochefoucault, Bolingbroke and Chesterfield, until what may be termed the catastrophe and turning point of his life occurred.

CHAPTER X.

The Journal — Remarks on the plan of Union — Aphorisms — Various memoranda — Inscription — Recipes — Palace of the King of Portugal — Visit to England — Return to Portugal.

The singular incidents, the strange vicissitudes, in the lives of Frankland and of Agnes Surriage, seem to belong rather to the world of romance than to that of stern reality; and hence the truth of such remarkable events has often been called into question; but from the spring of 1755 to the close of life, the baronet kept a kind of journal, or diary,[1] which is now in the possession of the Massachusetts Historical Society, and which not only reveals the coming, but also in part substantiates the past events in his strange history. It is a rare and curious duodecimo of some 200 pages, written in his own hand, and containing an account of current expenses; items of business; memoranda of estates, recipes, etc., interspersed with moral and political maxims and reflections. It often refers to matters and things quite trivial in themselves; yet in doing this it presents even a more vivid picture of the journalist's every day life and of the manners and the fashion of the times in which he lived.

[1] It was presented to the Society, October 29, 1851, by Matthias Ellis, Esq., of Boston, and to the society I am greatly indebted for the use of it in the preparation of this work.

The Journal.

"1755. March 17.—Mr. Coles gathers anemone seed. Wrote by packet to mother; Park and Willis for shoes. Paid for shaving in full for this, and the next month, at 6 sesterces per month,—1m. 200 rea.[1] Nothing considerable can ever be done by the colonies in the present disturbed state. The plan of union as concerted by the commissioners at Albany, if carried into execution, would soon make a formidable people. Disinterested public spirited men of sense who are versed in the nature of government, do believe that no objection can be made to it, but what makes against all kinds of government, the English more especially. The prerogatives, the rights of the people, are therein both preserved without the least infringement the one upon the other.[2]

---

[1] 1000 reas = 1 milrea. 13½ reas = 1 English penny. The moidore of Portugal equals £1, 7*s.* sterling.—*Dilworth's Arith.*, p. 83.

[2] The French had already extended a line of forts along the great lakes, the Ohio and Mississippi rivers, as far as the Gulf of Mexico, and were making daily encroachments upon the territory in possession of the English. A convention of the thirteen colonies was therefore held at Albany, June 9, 1754, for the purpose of devising a plan of union against the common enemy. The plan proposed by Franklin and adopted by the convention, July 4th, was that the general government should be administered by a president general, appointed and supported by the crown, and a grand council of forty chosen by the representatives of the people of the several colonies. "It is not altogether to my mind," said Franklin, "but it is as good as I could get it."—*Bancroft*, vol. IV, p. 125. — The colonies opposed it lest it might infringe their rights; the king, because it gave them too much power; so between the two it fell.

The uneasiness thou feelest; the misfortunes thou bewailest; behold the root from which they spring, even thine own folly, thine own pride, thine own distempered fancy. Of much speaking cometh repentance; but in silence is safety. Put a bridle on thy tongue, set a guard on thy lips, lest the words of thine own mouth destroy thy peace.

Notata. A noble spirit disdaineth the malice of fortune, the greatness of his soul is not to be cast down.

A fool is provoked with insolent speeches; but a wise man laugheth them to scorn.

In all thy desires, let reason go along with thee; and fix not thy hope beyond the bounds of probability, so shall success attend thy undertakings, and thy heart shall not be vexed with disappointments.

March 19.—Went to Sagavan with Mr. Horne.

20.—Cash Dr. to John Airey—received of him on account 20 moidores, . . 96.000

House expenses Dr. to cash:

1 Pair silk stockings, ...	2.700
Washerwoman, ...	680
1 Pair French shoes, ...	1.300
A tippet, ...	800
Total expended this week, .	6.680

21.—To go to Mrs. Brown's to see a procession.

23.—Went on horseback to Don Pedro's Infanta.

24.—Overturned in chaise.

To a poor man, . . . - . 240

To six pair of gloves for woman, . 1.080

27.—Was at the court to see the king wash the poor men's feet.

28.—To the tailor's account, . 14.560

29.—Paid the baker for 42 loaves at 40 rea each, ... 1.680

For washing, 540; charges at Panada,. . . . . 6,400=6.940

Food as per Jacinta's account, laid out by him in all March, . . 45.280

Total this week, 23.280

3d, ... 6.680

Total, 75.140

April 1.—Returned from Colares.[1]

4.—Farrier for currying macho.[2] 1.200

Chaise hire. 1.200

Paid for a peruque.

Jacinta's wife for mending shirts, etc., ... 2.180

Paid Mr. Coles in full, for four months lodging, due this day, . 128.000

Cash debtor to Thomas Horne, . 128.000

5.—Went to Cintra.[3]

---

[1] Colares, celebrated for its wine, lies in a beautiful valley near Cintra, about a league from the Rock of Lisbon, and 20 miles from the city itself.

[2] The Portuguese word for horse.

[3] Cintra stands quite picturesquely at the foot of a rocky mountain, 14 miles from Lisbon, and contains about 4,000 inhabitants. It enjoys a charming prospect of the verdant valley of Colares, of the great monastery of Mafra, and of the ocean. It is the favorite summer resort of the nobility and the rich merchants of Lisbon. William Beckford, Esq., the wealthy author of *Vathek*, had a

April 7.—Returned from Cintra to Lisbon.

8.—Paid peruque maker for combing wigs for 3 months, . . . 7.200

For boy. 240,—charges at Panada. 480 = 620

For chaise hire, 5.400; chaise man, 400 = 5.800

For singing man. 480; Mr. Horne's servant, ... 480 = 960

9.—Went to opera.

To milkman at 40 rea per pint, . 1.080

11.—To putting a new glass to the chaise, ... 3.200

Paid baker—32 loaves, . . 1.280

For borders 3 feet wide, Persian ranunculus, paracelsus, jonquils, red Turkey, yellow do., belladonna, lily.

1715. April 16.—To Jacinta, . 480

---

palace at Cintra, and Southey dates his *Thalaba* at this place, where he was living in 1800. It is thus graphically described in *Childe Harold*, Canto, I:

"Lo! Cintra's glorious Eden intervenes
In variegated maze of mount and glen.
* * * * *
The horrid crags, by toppling convent crown'd,
The cork-trees hoar that clothe the shaggy steep,
The mountain-moss by scorching skies imbrowned,
The sunken glen, whose sunless shrubs must weep,
The tender azure of the unruffled deep,
The orange tints that gild the greenest bough,
The torrents that from cliff to valley leap,
The vine on high, the willow branch below,
Mixed in one mighty scene, with varied beauty glow."

April, 22.—To Jacinta, 6.400. To Bacchus and Hannah[1] 1.600.

23.—Began to take diet drink.

24.—Sent macho to Verde at Mr. Morley's.[2]

25.—Transcribed from a stone pillar at Penneverde in Portugal.

SOLUTIS	also	SALVOS IRE,
VOTIS		SUSCEPTIS
SALVOS		VOTIS SAL
REDIRE		VOS IRE.[4]
SALVOS		
REDIRE.[3]		[1543].

26.—To baker for 36 loaves 1.400.
For attiring peruque 800.
" 12 sheets of straw, postage at 100 rea each sheet.

Remarks on houses in Portugal:—The outside walls one story, ¾ of a yard and two inches; partition walls ¾ of a yard, less two inches.

27.—Went to the opera.[5]

---

[1] Slaves who were with him at Hopkinton.

[2] Joseph Morley aided the sufferers by the earthquake with his kind attentions and purse. See *Boston Gazette*, 1756.

[3] "Our vows performed we go in peace."

[4] "Our vows made, we go in peace."

[5] The opera at Lisbon was then the best in Europe.
Hist. Portugal.

At eve beneath the pictured dome
The gilded courtiers throng;
The broad moidores have cheated Rome
Of all her lords of song.
Agnes, by Dr. O. W. Holmes.

29.—Went to dine with Mr. Die.

30.—To Domingus on account. 480; water for all the month of April for the house. 940; for the stable. 850. Mr. Paine, a bookseller in Bishopgate street, near the south sea, sells flower roots for Mr. Coles.

May, 5. Receipt from Mr. Coles: Æthiops mineral, gum guaicum, crabs eyes, ana, each four drachms, camphira, one drachm, salt of steel, one drachm mix't with rob. of elder into an electuary. Take it at 10 A. M. and at night, the bigness of a nutmeg; and once a week take a dose of hiera picra.

Cash to John Airey, 15 moidores,	72.000.
Paid milkman, ...	800.

To make white washing:—Take some best stone lime in an earthen pot, to which put a little water and some common Lisbon oil, with some blue. N. B. The lime must be put into the water by little and little lest it boil up and hurt the eye.

12.—Remarks at the King of Portugal's palace called Mafra.[1] Went to see the Visconde de Ponte de Limas at Mafra, a pretty shady place. He was

[1] Mafra, containing about 1000 inhabitants, is about five miles N. W. of Lisbon. John V commenced a palace of white marble here, in 1717, which was completed in 1742, and is called the Escurial of Portugal. It is 770 feet in length; has 807 rooms, and 5200 windows. It is said that 10,000 troops may be reviewed on the roof of the building. The library is 300 feet long and contains 30,000 volumes.

ambassador in Spain. The king's palace at the entrance has fine marble statues of several saints. Infirmary very neat with Dutch tile. Suite of rooms 1100 palms, each palm nine inches. The king and queen's private chapel is marble; very grand altar pieces done by Ignatio de Olievira. The serenata, or music hall, fine; the library room large. Here follows a description of the convent, etc.

May 8.—Went to Mafra. One of the king's coaches at Lisbon cost 120,000 crowns. He has near 80 coaches.

June 3.—Went on board the Hanover packet at 7 in the evening.

" 16.—Arrive at Falmouth in England.

Cheerful, but not gay; serious but not grave, he drinketh the joys and sorrows of life with steadiness and serenity.

" 18.—Set out for Fareham.

" 20.—Arrived at Exeter. 22, Set out from Exeter to Fareham. 25, Arrived at Captain Gaylon's. 28, Start for Fareham. 29, Arrived in London.

July 6.—Came to my house in Clargis street.

Proceed not to speak, or to act, before thou hast weighed the words and examined the tendency of every step thou shalt take.

Aug. 17.—In England it was called a hot day: deg. by thermometer 64 at 9 A. M.

Terrify not thy soul with vain fears; neither let thy heart sink within thee from the phantoms of imagination.

Sept. 4.—Set out from London to Falmouth in order to proceed to Lisbon.

CHAPTER XI.

Earthquake at Lisbon, 1755 — Description of the city — Effects of the Earthquake — Destruction of Life — Escape of the King — Benefaction of England.

The first day of November, 1755, will be ever memorable for the most violent and destructive earthquake of modern times. The seat of volcanic action seems to have been a little to the west of Portugal, and the successive shocks were so tremendous as to agitate an area of the earth's surface equal to seven and a half million square miles.[1] The most terrible destruction, however, occurred at Lisbon, which was near the centre of the cosmical disturbance. This city stands as Rome, on seven hills, which rise magnificently from the right bank of the Tagus, here about three miles wide, and form a kind of semicircle, crowded with costly private dwellings, stores, churches, palaces built of white marble, and presenting to the eye of an observer from the bay below one of the most enchanting prospects in the world. It had in 1755 almost a quarter of a million people, and was the residence of the richest king in Europe; even then the poet might truly say concerning it:—

> "Chi non a vista Lisboa
> Non a vista cosa boa."

[1] The shock was felt all over Western Europe, Northern Africa, and even to the West Indies. See *Lyell's Geology*, vol. II, p. 239.

The morning of the dreadful day was exceedingly fine; the sun rose with unusual splendor and bathed the summit of the hills, the spires and domes and pinnacles of the city in golden light. The sky was serene and clear, the winds were hushed, the sails hung lazily from the vessels in the Tagus, whose blue waters, as a burnished mirror, held the image of the town, the groves, the azure vault of heaven, deep in its bosom, undisturbed. It was All-saints-day;—day of imposing ceremony and festivity for the Roman church, but opening so calm and fair withal, that no one in the joyous city has the slightest dream of the irresistible agencies at work beneath him, or of the direful shock about to come. The bells peal forth their merry chimes; the streets are crowded with carriages and people of both sexes, gaily dressed; priest, noble, lady, tradesman, soldier, sailor, negro — every thing that goes to make up a vast city, — moving toward the various churches for the celebration of high mass. It is nearly ten o'clock; the bells have become silent; the people are kneeling in the temples and the priests proceeding with the services, when suddenly, a dreadful sound is heard, as pealing thunder from the bosom of the earth. The solid walls are shaking, and *misericordia* [1] rises from ten thousand

[1] "The terror of the people was beyond description; nobody cried; it was beyond tears. They ran hither and thither delirious with horror and astonishment, beating their breasts and faces, and crying *misericordia.*" Farme's *Account of the late dreadful Earthquake at Lisbon.*, p. 5.

whitened lips. A moment afterwards, another shock breaks the awful silence, and the fear is realized. The foundations are loosened; the lofty domes and towers of palace,[1] church, inquisition, topple to and fro: the solid masonry gives way, and with terrific crash the massive piles come plunging down, burying the affrighted people in one common grave. The sun is darkened,[2] the streets are filled with the dead and dying, crushed beneath the fragments of the falling houses; men, women and children are flying frantic every way, as if the day of general doom were come. The earth shakes and trembles for the space of twenty minutes like some living monster; the waters of the Tagus roll into the sea, leaving the vessels on the naked ground; and then come foaming, rushing back, *cumulo præruptus aquæmons,* and sweep the crowd of frantic people gathered on the new and spacious marble quay to quick destruction. The quay[3] itself goes down never to rise again. So violent are the shocks that by ten o'clock of that fatal Saturday the splendid palace of the king, the custom house, India house,

---

[1] "The Palace," says Mr. wolfall, "tumbled the first shock, but the natives insist that the Inquisition was the first building that fell."

[2] La poussière ètait si grande que le soleil en ètait obscurci. *Francesco Manoel.*

[3] "A sudden convulsion of the stream turned this pier bottom uppermost, like a ship on its keel in the tempest, and then engulphed it; and of all the living creatures who had lately thronged it full 3000, it is said not one even as a corpse ever rose again." Lord Mahon's *Hist., of England,* vol., IV, p. 61.

new opera houses, as many as thirty churches,[1] and almost all the stores and dwelling houses, are in ruins, [2] and nearly thirty thousand [3] people are crushed and killed beneath them. As if to add to the horror of this dreadful scene the prisoners are let loose, and then incendiary fires spring up on every hand, which, quickened by the rising tempest, threaten to consume whatever the convulsion of the earth has spared.

Touched by the finger of the Almighty, a gay, voluptuous, guilty city is in a moment left smouldering in ruins, and the royal command once more impressed upon the thoughtless world: "Be still and know that I am God!" The king and his court being at Belem,[4] during the earthquake, were saved; yet several persons of distinction, as the Spanish ambassador, the marchioness of Lourical, etc., perished; and in the letters written home to England after this catastrophe we have such sad details as these: "Mr. Hake's house fell the first shock and buried poor Mrs. Hake; Mr. John Churchill and Mr. Giles Vincent are killed. Mr. Chase was dug out of the ruins with both legs broken." Writing to his sister, the queen of Spain, the king[5] of Portugal

[1] The English church was the only one left standing.

[2] The loss of property was estimated at 2,284,000,000 francs.

[3] See *Lord Mahon's Hist., of England*, vol. IV, p. 62. Rees's *Encyclopedia* says 30,000 to 40,000. Rev. Mr. Davy, an eye-witness, says 60,000.

[4] Belem, Anglais Bethlehem, is about a mile south west of Lisbon. It is the Westminster of that city.

[5] Don Jose.

says; "Here I am, a king[1] without a capital, without subjects, without raiment." On asking Gen. Pedro d'Almeida what he ought to do, the very appropriate reply was given: Sire, enterrez les morts, songez aux vivants, fermez les portes. He acquiesced and set himself at once at work. It took him a long time, however, to bury the dead. England generously gave him £100,000 towards aiding the survivors; and the gates were not only closed upon the prisoners, but the bodies of two hundred of those who had been engaged in pillage and incendiarism were soon observed suspended upon gibbets around the city.

---

[1] Proclaimed king Sept. 7, 1750, and died 1777. An attempt was made on his life, Sept. 3,1758, while on his way to Belem to visit the beautiful marchioness Tavoro. Ten persons were executed for this deed, Jan. 13, 1759, and . the church of Sän Jose erected on the spot in 1760. Pombal, the Richelieu of Portugal, is thought to have been the secret instigator of the whole affair.

CHAPTER XII.

Frankland is buried in the ruins — His repentance — His release by Agnes Surriage — His marriage — Remarks upon the Earthquake — Effects of the calamity upon the people.

Frankland had returned to Lisbon, and had gone out upon the morning of the fatal day in his court dress to witness the celebration of high mass. He was riding with a lady, and happened to be passing, at about 40 minutes past ten o'clock, the house of Francesco de Ribeiro, when suddenly the earth begins to rise and sink like a wave at sea, the walls of contiguous buildings totter, bend and break over him, involving horses, carriage, and its occupants in the ruins.

The horses are killed instantly; and such is the agony of his companion, that she bites entirely through the sleeve of his red broad cloth coat, and tears a piece of flesh out of his arm. Entombed beneath a mass of broken timber, rocks and lime, and in immediate expectation of a most appalling death,[1]

[1] In a letter from an English merchant, dated on board the Swithington in the Tagus, Nov. 3, 1755, brought to Boston by Captain Joseph Inches, and published in the *Boston Gazette* Jan. 12, 1756, the writer says: "Sir Henry Frankland, I am told, escaped miraculously; he was in his chaise, and the moment he stepped out a house fell on it and buried the chaise, beasts and servants; he and lady are now at Belem." This in part is incorrect, as Frankland himself writes in his journal: "I was buried in ruins;" and Noble, in his *Memoirs of the House of Cromwell*, published in

Frankland begs for mercy; and his sins,— which are not a few, come rushing with most terrible distinctness into memory, and just on the brink of the eternal world, he makes a solemn vow to God, if he will show him pity, to lead henceforth a better life, and especially to atone for wrongs done Agnes Surriage, by making her his lawful, wedded wife.

Meanwhile she herself sets out in earnest search for him; and making her way along the narrow streets, now filled with the smouldering ruins, she fortunately comes to the very spot where he lies buried. She hears the smothered accents of his well known voice; she holds out large rewards to men for his recovery, and in the course of an hour or so, succeeds in rescuing him from the horrors of his living tomb.[1] He is carried into a house near by, his wounds are dressed, and after a little he is removed to Belem. Here, faithful to his vow, he leads his fair deliverer—and may we not well sup-

---

1787, states that Frankland was buried for an hour under the ruins of the great earthquake at Lisbon. Abram Castres Esq., the English envoy to the King of Portugal, says in a letter dated Lisbon, Nov. 6, 1755: "I must not forget to acquaint you that Sir Henry Frankland and Lady are safe and well." See *Gentlemen's Magazine*, 1756.

The *Boston Gazette*, Dec. 22, 1755, states on the authority of captain Collins, just arrived, that "during the shock of the dreadful earthquake, Sir Henry Frankland [formerly of this town] was saved, but the greater part of his family, if not all, perished in the ruins." This must have referred to the inmates of the house he lived in, which was destroyed.

[1] From Mrs. Swain by Mrs. Hildreth; Mrs. P. Bixby [Jennie Surriage] by the writer's mother; and from Isaac Surriage by Mrs. Dawes and others.

pose with tears of gratitude—to the hymeneal altar. The rite is solemnized, of necessity, by a Romish priest, and Agnes Surriage rises through the ruins of a city and her own to take the honored name of Lady Agnes Frankland.

Perhaps of all natural phenomena an earthquake is the most sublime and terrible. Originating in the intense action of those pent up and mysterious fires and gaseous elements which rage continually underneath the crust of the earth's surface; coming on suddenly with awful subterranean groans, with shock after shock so mighty as to rend and level the proudest structures man can rear to their foundations; so tremendous as to move the solid mountains and to sink whole cities in the sea, an earthquake, such as occurred at Lisbon, seems to portend and represent more fearfully than any other action of the physical forces the final dissolution of the globe itself. The very fact that the law is concealed, the hand invisible, moving in mystery, goes to augment the terror.[1]

The whole kingdom of Portugal was checked in its mad career by this stern rebuke of God; the public mind was sobered; theatres and other places of amusement were shut up, and the inquisition red with crime, was soon abolished. Even London was led to close her masquerades lest the continuance of such diversions might bring upon it a

[1] For theories respecting the action of telluric forces and phenomena of earthquakes, consult Sir Charles Lyell's *Principles of Geology*, also Mr. Robert Mallet's *Reports*.

similar calamity. The great lesson was needed; for the unsound philosophy of Shaftsbury, Bolingbroke and Chesterfield; of D'Alembert, Diderot, and Voltaire, was undermining public morality; and religion among the great had to an alarming extent degenerated from the inward spirit to the outward form. The voice of God through nature, as well as through the eloquent lips of Charles Wesley and George Whitfield, was wanting to arrest the tide; and in some degree it proved effectual. Frankland's spirit was chastened and subdued by the event. He recognized at once the hand of God in it; he changed his course and his philosophy. The record which he makes of the catastrophe and his excellent reflections thereupon, will, I think, awaken lively interest in one of the many mental revolutions which that sad All-saints-day effected.

CHAPTER XIII.

The Journal — Record of Frankland's escape — His reflections upon the earthquake — Extracts from the Records of the 2d church in Marblehead — Frankland revisits England — Cordial reception of his Lady — Returns again to Lisbon — Accounts and recipes.

JOURNAL.

1755. Nov. Durng my residence in Portugal happened the great earthquake, on which day I was providentially saved. I was buried in ruins. Francesco de Ribeiro lived in the house I was saved in at the time of the earthquake. Hope my providential escape will have a lasting good effect upon my mind.

We should endeavor to pacify the divine wrath by sorrow for past neglects and a future conscientious discharge of our duty to God and our country.

Natural calamities entirely proceed from the hand of God, and they are designed by providence as warnings to teach the inhabitants of the world righteousness. To imagine that any thing gives trouble to God, is attempting to measure infinity with the span of man's own hand and making God altogether such an one as ourselves. For suppose any man present at the late dreadful earthquake, and that he had it in his power without pain, or trouble to himself, to have relieved the wretched sufferers what would the world have thought of him, or what would he thought of himself, if he had not relieved them? and will he suppose the God of all nature less merciful than himself? or that he stood by a cruel spectator of the misery of his creatures, when with a word he could have caused the earthquake to cease, if he had not wise ends of his providence to serve by inflicting, or permitting the calamity?

It cannot reasonably be supposed that when God created the world by an absolute decree, he so fixed the laws of his creation as to reserve to himself no power to direct and overrule them, so as to make them subservient to the good of his providence. It is certainly far more agreeable to all our ideas of the majesty and perfections of God to consider him as presiding over the system of the world and employing the whole creation to execute the designs either of mercy, or of punishment.

No words can express the horror and destruction of that day's calamity. Your own thoughts must assist you in representing it to yourself. How dreadful to reflect; a great and populous city, as it were, in a moment cast down, and laid waste, with all its pride and glory sunk into one general ruin. Bring the reflection home to yourself and consider how great would be your consternation to feel the earth shaking from its centre;—to see every thing falling around you, houses, churches, palaces;—to have no hopes, but in flying from your danger, and yet to have no place of refuge to fly for security; to hear the cries and groans of the dying; to see the distresses of thousands made miserable and wretched for the loss of their friends and children.

The house in which Frankland resided was destroyed; slight shocks of the earthquake continued to occur and he therefore seized the first opportunity to embark with his lady for England. In order to make his marriage doubly sure, he had the ceremony again performed on board the ship[1] by a clergyman of his own church. On his arrival he introduced the lady Agnes to his mother who received her cordially as a daughter, who had doubly saved her son; and the other members of the family recognizing her rank, her beauty, and her elegant manners, made up, as it were, for past neglect by generous welcome and by many special tokens of esteem. It certainly was a triumph and a fortune such as this world seldom witnesses, that the daughter of a poor fisherman of Marblehead, should come by such strange circumstances to move in the aristocratic circles of the Franklands, Pelhams, Scarboroughs, Pitts and Walpoles, which at that period exercised such influence over the destinies of the most powerful empire in the world.

As soon as the condition of Lisbon would permit, Frankland returned to it and resumed his journal.

[1] "On enquiry it appears that Sir Henry married her on board ship during his voyage from Lisbon to England and that she was respected by his family at home." Miss T. T. Whinyates, in letter to me dated, Cheltenham, England, Sept. 13th, 1858.

1756. April. — Don Gaston's house in Portugal. Delivered to the care of Anne Foley, our housekeeper, 21 table cloths; 24 napkins; 24 towels.

Records from the 2d church in Marblehead: my wife was baptised by the Rev. Mr. Edward Holyoke, the pastor of the said church, in name of Agnes Surriage.

Commissioners of customs. Sir John Evelyn, Messrs Cavendish, Hotham, Vaugn, Westby, Mead, Levinz, Hooper, Tash.

April. 26.—Wrote to Sheaffe, Griffin, Mrs. Swain,[1] Mrs. M'Clelland and Dea Pearce.

Paid house rent for the month of April to Don Gaston's order 40.000.

To send Mr. Coles some asparagus seed, some cranberries, and some currant cuttings.

Sailed from Belem to Boston on board the ship Friendship, Captain Eleazer Johnson.

The largest sort of pigeons come from Pisa in Italy. N. B. The broken piece of the tea kettle stand is in my desk.

Mem.

To twist cotton for lamps. Take the cotton at both ends and twist it; then hold the middle in your mouth and double it; hold the two ends in your fingers and take it from your mouth, it will

[1] Lady Frankland's sister then living, as I suppose, at Hopkinton.

join itself. If you want it thicker, do the same again.

Mem.

Burn onions with a red hot iron at the roots and it will prevent them from growing and preserve them a long time from rotting.

Mem.

Sundries from Lisbon. Carnation seed, pink and crabo de salohia seed, scabious, onion seed from Montomor. To write to Mr. Mays and Majendie to send me a receipt, how they cured their Matanchia hams. Large panellas for soup; do. smaller. A set of dressing boxes — tippets.

At sea.

When you fry cod fish, cut the tail part horizontally and flour it well; dry it first. Indian meal.

CHAPTER XIV.

Arrival in Boston — Purchase of the Clarke mansion — Description of the same — His life in it — Various memoranda — Narrow escape.

Frankland arrived at Boston in the summer of this year and introduced to his compeers the lovely and accomplished, but once contemned and slighted, Agnes Surriage as Lady Frankland, who was at once recognized as a star of the first magnitude in the polished circles of the town.

The knight was too much occupied on his arrival in attending to the affairs of his office; in visiting his beautiful domains at Hopkinton, and in obtaining a suitable residence in Boston to attend to journalizing, and we have therefore, for some time only the following brief entries in this diary.

Aug. Boston. Gooding at Charlestown cabinet maker.

" 22. This day very hot, degree 92.

" 25. Degree at half past 12 P. M. 82.

" " Sally M'Clester[1] is 17 years of age the 25th of March, 1757.

On the 5th of October of this year, Frankland

[1] Daughter of his wife's sister, Mrs. Mary Swain, and afterwards the wife of John Dupee.

purchased of Mr. Thomas Greenough, instrument maker, for the sum of £1200 sterling, the celebrated Clarke[1] mansion on Garden Court street and Bell alley, at the north end of the town.

This house was erected by one of the wealthiest merchants in Boston, and was intended to rival in splendor the far-famed Hutchinson[3] house adjoining it. The site was beautiful and the house itself for that period was elegant and commodious. It was built of brick, three stories high, and contained in all twenty-six rooms. A spacious hall run through the centre from which arose a flight of stairs, so broad and easy of ascent that Frankland used to ride his pony up and down with ease and safety. The parlors were ornamented with fluted columns elaborately carved, and richly gilded pilasters and cornices; the walls were wainscotted and the panels embellished with beautiful landscape scenery; the mantel pieces were of Italian marble, and the fire places of the finest porcelain, which exhibited views of singular excellence. The floor of the eastern parlor was laid in diamond shaped figures, and had in the centre a unique and curious tessellated de-

[1] Benjamin Clarke, Esq., merchant, and Rebecca Winslow, children of Wm. Clarke, sold this estate to Thomas Greenough, Jan. 6, 1746-7 for £1400, old tenor.— *Suffolk Deeds.*

[2] There is a pleasant story by Miss Leslie of a visit of Benjamin Franklin to this house when a newsboy. — See *Violet.* Philadelphia, 1839. It is described in Cooper's *Lionel Lincoln;* although incorrectly said to stand in Tremont street.

[3] This house was mobbed by the populace, August 26, 1765, and damaged to the amount of £2,500. The wines of the comptroller of customs were in the cellar and greatly inflamed the mob. I do not learn that Frankland's house was injured.

sign, consisting, it is said, of more than three hundred different kinds of wood, as mahogany, ebony, satin wood, etc., encircling the coat of arms of the Clarke family.[1]

To this elegant mansion, furnished with regal splendor, the baronet introduced his lady, and here, during the winter seasons, she presided over the élite of the court end of the town, as one of the most elegant and charming women of that period. But though Lady Frankland had thus risen from obscurity to this commanding social position, she did not allow herself to forget her humble origin; or cease to cherish a sister's kind regard for the other members of her family. She received and supported Sarah and John M'Clester, her sister Mary's children; and her brother, Isaac Surriage, seaman, always found a hearty welcome to her hospitable mansion. The following entries in the collector's diary are full of interest, as exhibiting something, not only of the daily life of this remarkable family, but also of the manners and customs of those old colonial times.

1756. Oct. 23. Harry Cromwell went to Piscataqua with Capt. M'Daniel in order to go on board his majesty's ship, Success, Capt. Rouse,[2] at Casco Bay.

[1] Now preserved in a beautiful table in possession of Roland Ellis, Esq.

[2] John Rouse, a particular friend of Frankland, commanded the *Shirley*, 24 guns, which carried General Pepperrell to Louisbourg. He carried the news of the capture of that fortress to England, and was made captain in R. N., Sept. 24, 1745. He was changed to the *Success*, 22 guns, in 1756. He commanded the *Sutherland*,

Harry Cromwell is 16 years of age next February.

Oct. 27. Laid in 40 bushels of oats.

" 31. Hired Charles at the rate of £150, per annum, old tenor.

No. of acres of land at Hopkinton that pays quit rent to the college, Gooch 271; Hobbs 77; Preston 50: 398.

Nov. 3. Paid milk man.

Dec. 4. Paid Robert £36.[1]

" " Paid milk man, £3 5*s*; baker £7 5*s*.

" 17. A great snow storm.

" 30. Col. Pollard[2] was buried. Mrs. Villiers[3] came from Hopkinton. Mr. Stoddard,[4] Mrs. and Miss Sally and Nelly Stoddard; Mrs. Brimsden and Mr. and Mrs. Greenough supped with us.

" 31. Drew an order on Deblois, senior, to pay Mrs. Fletcher 175 old tenor; viz., Marseilles quilt £110; for a screw £65: £175.

Jan. 1. Paid off old milk man; paid Mr. Auch-

---

50 guns, 1759, from which vessel, Gen. Wolfe issued his last orders before ascending the heights of Abraham. He died at Portsmouth, N. H., April 3, 1760. — See *Col. Hist. N. Y.*, Vol. X, p. 60, note, by Dr. O'Callaghan.

[1] He was with him at Lisbon.

[2] Col. Benjamin Pollard was high sheriff of Boston for 13 years. He commanded the Cadets, and introduced the bayonet into the Province. He was elected member of the ancient and honorable Artillery Co., 1726, and died December 24, 1756, aged 61. — See *Hist. An. and Hon. Arty. Co.*, by Z. G. Whitman.

[3] See page 80.

[4] Captain Thomas Stoddard died April 12, 1663, aet. 64 and was buried on Copp's Hill, where his headstone may still be seen.

muty,[1] £23. Mr. and Mrs. Sheaffe [2] supped with us. Paid Johnny's school mistress.[3]

Jan. 4. Gave manufacturer of stair carpet £5.

" 11. Mrs. Hill and Deblois dined with us.

" 14. Mrs. Ellis came to us. Paid my barber one quarter's shaving at £6 per year. To examine books 1740, bill of exchange for £25 drawn by me.

" 17. Paid the baker £8 12*s*.

" 18. Paid for two loads of country walnut wood, £7, old tenor.

" 26. Mr. and Mrs. Trevellet; Mrs. Inman;[4]

---

[1] This was Robert Auchmuty, the younger, whose sister, Elizabeth, married John Overing, Esq. He left America in 1776, and died in England.

[2] Their daughter, Susan, married Captain Molesworth of the 29th regt. 1761.

[3] John M'Clester, son of Lady Frankland's sister.

[4] Ralph Inman had a store on Green's wharf, 1763. His house, a venerable mansion on a commanding site in Cambridgeport, is still standing. It was once the head quarters of Gen. Putnam.— See Col. Swett's *Bunker Hill Battle*, p. 9. He was a friend of Frankland, and had charge of his property after he left this country, as may be seen by the following advertisement:— To be leased for a term of years, and entered upon the 25th March next, a farm at Hopkinton, suitable for a gentleman or farmer, belonging to Sir Henry Frankland, Bart., now tenanted by Joseph Villiers. Any person that inclines to hire the same may apply to Ralph Inman at his house in Cambridge, or his warehouse in Boston. *Boston Evening Post*, Jan. 7, 1765. To be let the mansion house of Sir Henry Frankland, Bart., adjoining His Honor's the Lieut. Governor's. Any person that inclines to hire the same may apply to Ralph Inman. *Boston Evening Post*, July 29, 1765.

Rowe; Davis and husbands, and Judge Tasker[1] supped with us.

[The 2d of Oct. 1756 came to my house, the 4th, signed the writings.]

Jan. 29. Capt. Rouse arrived from Halifax with Gov. Lawrence.

" 31. Paid milk man 43 qts. £2.13*s*.

Feb. " John Cole, merchant in Providence, recommended by Mr. Troutbeck.

" 11. Capt. Winfield has a curious sword fish. The best flour from York is marked G. V. R. and marked X on the bildge. Steward, a carter, over against the hay market; a maid that lived with Curtis. Mr. Charles Little entered the service, June 1747. Mrs. Hill, Lewis, Deblois, Mrs. Sheaffe, etc., dined with us.

" 12. Bought a side of mutton, weight 39½ lbs. We cut open the back, 1¾ inches fat; between the legs 3¼ inches fat. Cost 3*s*. old tenor.

" 18. Paid Bill, Butcher, per order on Sheaffe, £16, 1*s*. 9¼d. Mr. Sheaffe Dr. to me for what he sent the admiral, charged on said account per bill.

" 23. Paid the Baker.

" 28. Supped with Captain Davis. Mrs. Read, about half a mile from Weymouth meeting house, the lower road, sells excellent cheese at 3*s*. per pound.

Mar. 12. Bought a quarter of beef, weight 274 *lbs*. at 22*d*. of Mr. Bell. Sent in Saturday 74 *lbs*. at 20*d*.

---

[1] He was of Marblehead and judge of Essex Co., from 1755 till his death in 1761.— See *Washburn's Jud. Hist. Mass.*, p. 52.

Mar. 17. Dr. Cutler[1] gave me a tree called Catalpa. Account of Custom House fees received by Mr. Sheaffe, 1757. Received in January, £432 5*s.* Feb. £461 17*s.* 6*d.*, March, £354.

July 8. Felt a small earthquake at 25 minutes after two in the afternoon.[2]

" 9. Hired Thomas, French cook, at 15 dollars per month.

In August of this year the baronet and his lady narrowly escaped injury on their way, as I suppose, from Hopkinton to Boston. The account of it I find in the *New Hampshire Gazette*, Sept. 2, 1757. "Boston Aug. 20, 1757. Thursday last as Sir Henry Frankland and his lady were coming into town in their chariot, a number of boys were gunning on Boston neck [notwithstanding there is an express law to the contrary] when one of them discharging his piece at a bird, missed the same, and almost the whole charge of shot came into the chariot where Sir Henry and his lady were, several of which entered his hat and clothes, and one grazed his face, but did no other damage to him or lady."

Sept. 2. Paid Thomas, cook, 15 dollars; £482 due to Sally. Jarvis, Cahill and Co. arrived from London.[3]

" 20. Wrote to Fanny Russell, my sister; Stan-

[1] Dr. Timothy Cutler, 1st Rector of Christ's Church, Boston, was settled Dec. 29, 1723, and died August 17, 1765, at the advanced age of 82.

[2] "1757 July 8, 15 minutes past 2, an earthquake." Lewis's *Hist. Lynn.*

[3] Sept. 14, 1757. Frankland buys a lot of land on Sun Court St. for £113 6*s.* 8*d*, of Robert Jenkins. See *Suffolk Reg.* Deeds.

ly, Roberts, Capt. Howard and Mrs. Stainforth. A consul should endeavor to obtain weight and influence in the tribunals of Portugal.

Oct. 14. Paid Hutchinson[1] for beer and fish. Mass. Bay had on the alarm list 4,500 to bear arms; training list 3,200. Write to Mrs. Fanny Russell, my sister.

" 22. Wrote to Mrs. Stanley by Captain Kirkwood, and sent 2½ barrels of cranberries; one to Mr. Wood; the other to Mrs. Stanley.

Mrs. Eben Storer, camera, electrical machine, microscope.[2] Cranberries for Fanny Russell, Mrs. Stainforth, Mr. Wood, Mr. Stanley, Mrs. Wright, Mr. Pelham, Ld. Northumberland.

" 28. Sent four half barrels of cranberries per Capt. Cahill and four per Capt. C. Gasmay to the above persons, to the care of Mr. Stanley. Wrote to Stanley per Gasmay and Cahill. Capt. Peter Collyn was poisoned, on the coast of Guinea, by the negroes, many years ago. James Collyn, his own brother, lives at Rhode Island, goes to sea, has two sons, Peter and James; has two sisters in Boston, one a widow of Dr. Ranchan, and one unmarried, about 54 years old. They keep a school in Seven star[3] lane, near Trinity church. 482 sterling due to Sally.

---

[1] Gov. Thomas Hutchinson, his nearest neighbor. Bancroft says [*Hist.*, vol. IV, p. 27,] he so coveted money that he became a trader in his native town, and like others, smuggled goods which he sold at retail.

[2] Probably the articles mentioned before as given to H. C. in 1757.

[3] Now Summer street.

CHAPTER XV.

Appointed Consul General of Portugal — Prepares to leave Boston — Arrives at Lisbon — J. J. Villiers in charge of his place at Hopkinton — Don Pedro's maxim — Visit of Lord Kennoul to Lisbon — Marriage of the Princess of Brazil.

1757. As Frankland had by his former residence in Portugal become well acquainted with its language and commercial regulations, and as his declining health demanded a milder clime than that of Boston, he sought and obtained, in July of this year, of King George the third, an appointment as consul general of that kingdom. His appointment is thus noticed in the *London Magazine.* "Sir Henry Frankland, bart., appointed consul general at Lisbon, July, 1757." Leaving therefore his estate at Hopkinton in the hands of Mr. Villiers; his affairs in Boston[1] with his friend Deblois, he resigns his office as collector of the customs, and makes, as will be seen by his diary, his preparations for visiting London and taking up his residence again in Portugal.

Nov. 25. Left with Mr. Deblois[1] my last will and testament, 5 lottery tickets, Mr. Smith's note for £30 sterling.

---

[1] Gilbert, Lewis and Stephen Deblois were owners of Concert Hall in 1754. Gilbert was warden of King's Chapel in 1769-1774. The Deblois were included in the absentee act.

JOURNAL.

Leave Hopkinton lands to Mr. Villiers and one note of hand for two pair of oxen sold him and a promissory obligation to make 180 rods of stone wall.

A large case containing one small box of china figures; India dressing case; silver tea chest; backgammon table with silver ewer and shaving bason; microscope, dessert ornaments, Chelsea china, one pair white netts for horses; parasol silk; Italian prints; paper, silver shaving bason, book of maps, silver knives and forks, boxes and wafers.

Mem. To purchase in London for Lisbon, silver castors; wine glasses like Pownal's; two turreens; saucers for water glasses, dessert knives and forks and spoons; common tea kettle; jelly and syllabub glasses; fire grate; long dishes; tea cups, etc., clothes, etc., for Lady Frankland. Consul's seal; combs; mahagony tray, press for table linen and sheets; stove for flat irons; glass for live flea for microscope; Hoyle's Treatise on Whist; Dr. Doddridge's Exposition on the New Testament, 16 handsome chairs, with 2 settees, and 2 card tables, working table like Mrs. F. F. Gardner's.

Nov. 25. Left with Mr. Deblois my last will and testament.

Dec. 10. Sent to uncle Richard by the snow, Capt. Hugh Hunter, Devonshire, 1 case canary. 1 do malaga, to Mr. Stanley; 1 do rum, to Mr. Stainforth.

Wm. Scott, Neptune, Organ. Number of lottery

tickets left with Deblois. No. 4173, 4174, 4177, 4178, 4179, [all blanks].[1]

Not to be frighted out of their privileges, and if Lord * * * was determined to deprive them of them by force, they could muster as many men as he in the province.

1758, Jan. Mem. To mention to the governor about Dr. Jones, to continue him. To get John Jones[2] 3d Captain in Col. Buckminster's regiment, deputy sheriff of the county of Middlesex in the room of Thomas Mellen, under Foster of Charlestown. To ask the governor, if Capt. Elisha Jones is to supercede Col. Buckminster, if he says, yes: to move that Maj. Jones should proceed before Elisha Jones. Col. Minot will not take up. Jones is major, and Minot is lieutenant governor. Elisha Jones is the youngest captain.

Set out from Boston to Piscataqua, in order to go to England, and came to Piscataqua,[3] Wednesday following. Lodge at Mr. Solly's.[4]

Feb. 7. Went on board the Mermaid at 6 o'clock P. M.

---

[1] The general court authorized the town, 1757, to raise £21,000 by a lottery, towards paving and repairing the neck.— Drake's *Hist. Boston*, p. 644.

[2] Afterwards Col. John Jones. He was one of the three sons of John Jones, Esq., and Hannah, daughter of Savill Simpson. A second was Dr. Simpson Jones, who married Hannah Gooch, Aug. 24, 1740. The other was Anthony. They were Frankland's neighbors at Hopkinton.

[3] Portsmouth.

[4] He was collector of Portsmouth and lived on Daniel street; the house is still standing.

Feb. 23. Sailed from Piscataqua in North America for England in the Mermaid,[1] man of war, Capt. Alexander Innis.

Mrs. Haman's receipt for costiveness; one spoonful of sulphur and oyl of sweet almonds mixt, to be taken over night.

Mr. G. Thomas Gunning in partnership with Mr. Osborne, steel merchant in Sheffield, Yorkshire, is going to Lisbon to settle a correspondence. Recommended by uncle Fred. to my countenance and protection.

Aug. 4. Came to my house near the crux de Talbaida.

Sept. 29. Gavazza, a good lawyer; perfects a pamphlet on the practice of gardening. £1116. 11*s.* 9*d.*, old tenor was due me from Sheaffe; since which he paid £2000 to Mr. Deblois. Due to me by Sheaffe by last account £30 sterling.

1759. We have but few traces of the life of Frankland in 1759; it is probable that he revisited Boston in the early part of the year, as I find by the court records that he bought [Feb. 28,] 81 acres of land of Jeremiah Hobbs of Hopkinton for £900 old tenor; his country seat in that town was, however, under the management of Mr. Villiers at this time and the purchase might have been made

[1] The same vessel which, under Captain Douglas, took the Vigilant, 560 men, May 18, 1745, and in which the Rev. Roger Price sailed to England in 1747. It was lost near the Bahamas, June 24, 1760.

by him. The Rev. Ebenezer Parkman,[1] of Westborough records a visit to this place in his diary, under date of April 9th, thus:

"I proceeded to Sir Harry Frankland's seat kept now by Mr. Jaques Joseph Villiers de Rohan, mariè avec Mademoiselle Frances de Turenne. He gave me such slips, branches, cions, and seeds as I desired; and lent me Du Moulin's book of ye Accomplishment of ye Prophecies, or Third Book of ye Defence of ye Catholique Faith. I borrowed it for ye sakes of a trial with my Mr. Blanc, for it being French, I presume not to read much of it."

On July 4th of this year, Frankland was at Lisbon, and the following entries occur in his journal.

Don Pedro's[2] maxim was that a prince might be very faithful to his allies without preferring their interests to his own. The allies overstrain the cord of their connexion with Don Pedro. The duke de Giovannazzo, the Spanish minister, was too hard for Don Pedro; for he vanquished like the Tartars, by flying. Mem. In Germany and Portugal, no lady of distinction will marry any man, unless he authentically make it appear that his ancestors have been gentlemen and equally married for ten generations.

Andre Montano genovaz, florest rua dos calaptes

---

[1] Minister of Westborough, Massachusetts, nearly 60 years. He was settled Oct. 28, 1724 and died Dec. 9, 1782. See Allen's *Biog. Dict. in loco.*

[2] Brother to the King, Don José.

junto ao palacio do conde de S. Tiago. To fold a great coat, lay it in small circumference; just spread it on the ground and double it square; then double from feet part to shoulder part, then the sides turn up about 3 feet each; then two persons roll up and tie it.

1760. Mr. Dearing and Mr. Pennick, acquaintances of uncle Fred. The 37 Ps., proper for a day of fasting for a continuance of success in war. The consequence of a battle is much the best rule to judge by and plainly shows which party has the advantage. The Brazils were discovered in the year 1500.

Feb. 8. The earl Kennoul,[1] ambassador extraordinary and plenipotentiary, landed at Lisbon at about 2 o'clock, P. M. Lamberti in regard to ceremonials for ambassadors, 14 vol.

April 21. Lord Kennoul set out for Cintra, with Lord Strathmore, Mr. Pitt,[2] Mr. and Mrs. Hay; Mr. Williamson, Mr. Francis,[3] and Mr. Fowler.

To make boots soft and leather subtle, rub them

---

[1] The object of Lord Kennoul's mission to the court of Portugal was to remove the misunderstanding between the two crowns in consequence of Admiral Boscawen's having destroyed some French ships under the Portuguese fort in the bay of Lagos.—See note to Horace Walpole's Correspondence, vol. IV, p. 5.

[2] This was Thomas, only son of Thomas Pitt of Boconnock, eldest brother of the famous William Pitt, afterwards Lord Camelford.

[3] Sir Philip Francis, born 1740, died 1818; one of the reputed authors of Junius.

a little distance from the fire with neats foot oyl with your hand.

June 5. The Infanta[1] Don Pedro was married to the princess of Brazil.

" 7, 8, 9. Illuminations in Lisbon on account of the marriage of Don Pedro and princess of Brazil.

" 15. The pope's nuncio[2] ordered to leave the kingdom of Portugal. Rub knives and forks, guns, etc. with linseed oyl to preserve from rust.

July 2. Wed. Lord Kennoul at Lisbon, made a great entertainment on account of the marriage between Don Pedro and the princess of Brazil. The Dutch will give up nothing that concerns their interest in point of trade.

---

[1] Doña Maria, who succeeded her father Don José, as queen of Portugal, May 13, 1777. She married her uncle Don Pedro.

[2] The Jesuits were expelled from Portugal by Pombal, the Richelieu of that kingdom.

CHAPTER XVI.

Summers at Caldas — Gen. Burgoyne at Lisbon — All in the Wrong — Weight of Sir Henry and Lady — His views of Cromwell — Recipes for Lady Frankland — Maxims — Return to England.

At the close of the festivities in honor of the marriage of Doña Maria to her uncle Don Pedro, in which Frankland and his lady prominently shared, they went to reside for the remainder of the summer, at Caldas de Rainha,[1] a fashionable resort for the invalids at Lisbon on account of its hot sulphur springs. It will be seen by his journal that Frankland spent several successive summers at this place, diverting himself with riding, hunting, botanizing, reading and playing whist and backgammon with Lady Frankland, Lucy Barclay, Edward Hay,[2] Mr. Jaffarys and other congenial friends. It is interesting to see his outfit for his visit to the springs.

Aug. Things necessary for journey to Caldas, viz: guns, powder, shot, rammer to wash guns, flints, shot pouches, powder horn, fine emery, neats foot oyl, turn screw, dog chains, and padlock, large powder flask, saddle and bridle for little macho, ditto for Lady Frankland, almanack, pens, ink, paper, memorandum book, almond powder, hammers, chisels, nails, corks.

---

[1] The temperature of the waters, which are impregnated with sulphureted hydrogen, is 92°F.

[2] Edward Hay, Esq., appointed Envoy Extraordinary to the king of Portugal, July 19, 1757.—*London Magazine*, July, 1757.

Aug. 2. 1760. Set out from Lisbon at midnight and got to Villa Nova at $5\frac{1}{2}$ in the morning. From Villa Nova to Sercal, 6 hours journey; from Sercal to Chinchieza, 3 hours 35 minutes; from Chinchieza to the Caldas at 10 minutes past 8 at night. The men's bath at Caldas is 46 palms long and 13 palms broad, and will contain 60 persons at a time.

Oct. 1. Came to Lisbon at 12 m. on Thursday.

Nov. 2. Lord Kennoul sailed for England on board the Isis.

" 17. Paid Mr. Edward Browne 3 moidores to remit to Miss Bean on account of butter. History of Health and Art of Preserving it by James Mackenzie.

Dec. 8. Col. Arnott, Mr. Lowrey and Burgoyne[1] from Gibralter dined with us.

---

[1] General John Burgoyne was the natural son of Lord Bingley. He commanded a body of troops sent to Portugal for its defence against the Spaniards in 1762. He married clandestinely Lady Charlotte Stanly, youngest daughter of Edward, 11th Earl of Derby. Defeated in 1777 by General Horatio Gates, he repaired to England, became a member of Parliament and afterwards commander in chief in Ireland and member of the Privy Council. He published the *Lord of the Manor*, 1781, the *Heiress*, 1786, the *Maid of the Oaks*, and other dramas.

The caustic Trumbull writes to him:

Then raise thy daring shouts sublime,
And dip thy conquering pen in rhyme,
And changing war for puns and jokes,
Write new Blockades, and Maids of Oaks.

McFingal, Canto, iv, p. 117.

He closed his eventful life, Aug. 4, 1792, and was buried in Westminster Abbey.

Dec. 12. In Portugal, a cloudy, cold, disagreeable day. In the house no fire. The degree by Bird's thermometer was 58.

1761. An account of the new Comedy called *All in the Wrong*, written by Mr. Murphy.[1] The general intention of this comedy is to point what infinite perplexities may arise in the conversation between the sexes both before and after marriage, from our readily giving way to unnecessary suspicions, even on strong appearances, without endeavoring by a cool and discreet conduct to come to such as may be necessary for the clearing up of our doubts and restoring that peace of mind which a contrary conduct must unavoidably destroy.

When a fashion has become almost universal, though it may appear ridiculous to you, it is best to comply, and not to appear too singular in your own opinion.

May 15. Degree of heat by thermometer at 4 o'clock, was 74.

> The rabble will in triumph rudely share,
> And kings the rudeness of their joy must bear.

June 29. Degree of heat at 3 P. M. was 85.

July 16. Arrived at Caldas at 7¼ in the evening.

---

[1] Arthur Murphy was born at Cork, Ireland, in 1727, and died in 1805. In addition to *All in the Wrong*, he wrote the *Grecian Daughter*, and the *Way to keep him*. *All in the Wrong*, came out in 1761 and met with considerable success; it is borrowed in part from Molière's *Le Cocu Imaginaire*. See Horace Walpole's Correspondence, vol. IV.

Aug. 7. Went to St. Martintro in company with Mrs. Barclay, Lucy, Mr. and Mrs. French, Lady Frankland and Compton, Mrs. Farmer and returned the 11th day.

" 18. Lady Frankland weighs, rove,	4.26
Mrs. Barclay.	4.09
Mrs. French.	4.28
Mrs. Farmer.[1]	3.30
Miss Lucy Barclay.	4.19
Sir H. Frankland.	4.14
Mr. Jaffareys.	5.31

N. B. a rove is 32 lb. weight.

Cromwell made religion a cloak to his ambitious designs. He made it his study to find out and employ men of courage and capacity. Cromwell had his faults; but it can never be denied that he was one of the greatest generals England *ever had.*

Nov. 22. Degree by Bird's thermometer at 3 P.M. was 61. Called in Portugal a cold day.

Jan. 19. Lord Bristol sailed for England in the Portland, Capt. Hughes.

Poultice for macho's hoof. Two quarts bran, boyled well and strained, oyl and lard, q. s. Four spoonfuls of honey spread on coarse cloth.

Feb. 7. Snowed, degree of thermometer 52.

March 21. Sent the old postilion beast and horse to grass at 12 verts each.

---

[1] Her husband wrote an account of the earthquake published in Boston, 1756.

March 24. Gen. Crawford[1] arrived at Lisbon in the Success, Capt. Traine.

Aug. 6. At Caldas. Dr. Wade's recipe for Lady Frankland, when she had a sore throat; to take two spoonfuls every two hours a little warm.

℞ decocti pectoralis, lb, ij, oxymel, simpl, ℥ iss. Nitri pur, ℥i. m.

Dr. Wade's gargle for Lady Frankland. Marsh mallows and figs boyled together, and then add a little milk; to gargle with it a little warm.

A purging draught ordered by Dr. Wade for Lady F. who was then ill of a violent cold and troubled with profuse sweats.

℞ manna opt. ℥i. Salis cathart. amari ʒij. Solv. in aq. font ℥ iv. Colat. exhib. in usum.

French Huguenots at Lisbon very prejudicial to the British trade.[2]

> Orus, quando ego te aspiciam? quandoque licebit,
> Ducere solicitæ jucunda oblivia vitæ?[3]

---

[1] England declared war against Spain, January 4, 1762, and Portugal followed her in May of the same year, the Spanish army having already crossed the frontiers. Lord Tyrawley held command of the English forces for a while; but soon returned to London, when the Earl of Loudoun took his place and entrusted the command of his army to Count LaLippe, Generals Burgoyne, Townshend, Crawford and others. See Lord Mahon's *Hist. of England*, vol. IV, p. 275.

[2] "C'était," says the king of Prussia, "le commerce lucratif que L'Angleterre faisait en Portugal que la France voulait ruiner." *Histoire de la Guerre de Sept Ans.*

[3] Hor. lib. II, Sat. 6.

At Portella there is a quinta with a most delightful prospect at 80 moidores per annum.

It is an error in politics, especially in regard to Portugal, to suffer any innovation, or infraction of treaty to pass unnoticed by the public minister abroad, or minister at home.

Men generally act consistently with their interest except their pleasure interfere.

Espinhaço, spina, dog's name. paid 3.200.

Nov. 1. Purge for Lady Frankland.

℞ mann, opt. ℥i.
Sal. Polychrest. ʒi.
Solv in aqua font. q. s.
Colat. exhib. in usum.

Nov. Lord Trelawney told Mr. H * * * that he did prostrate, not only the dignity, but the interest, of the nation.

" I never amuse others, or perhaps myself, with whispers, or common reports.

" My liverys made by Mr. Robinson cost 19.015 each, beside the cost of frogs for the coat, and lace for the waistcoat.

1763, Lisbon, April 11. Went to Mr. Coles at Cintra; returned from there the 16th, do. We were 4 hours and 20 minutes on the road.

Receipt to dress Montanjo hams. First wash them with milk warm water, then let them soak in cold water for about two hours and then roast them.

Aug. 9. Sailed from Lisbon in the Hanover packet, Capt. Sherburne and arrived at Falmouth on Wednesday, Aug. 17, 1763.

The best books to learn children to read English are, *A New Guide to the English Tongue*, by Thomas Dilworth;[1] *The Royal English Grammar*,[2] by James Greenwood; the *Spelling Dictionary* of the English language with a compendious English Grammar prefixed.

---

1 First published 1761. The author died 1780.

2 First published 1711. Favorably mentioned in the *Tattler*.

CHAPTER XVII.

Visit to America — Residence at Bath — Remark upon Sir Robert Walpole — Retires from public life — Style of living at Bath — Death — Monumental inscription — Character.

1763. On leaving Lisbon and London this year Sir Henry returned to Boston and Hopkinton, where he spent some time in viewing his beautiful grounds and entertaining his former friends and associates; but his health continuing to decline, he proceeded with his lady and Harry Cromwell to Bath, England, for the purpose of enjoying the benefit of its celebrated mineral waters. It appears that he sought here to obtain and enjoy the *otium cum dignitate* of a tranquil and philosophic old age.

1764. He says:

I endeavour to keep myself calm and sedate: I live modestly and avoid ostentation, decently, and not above my condition, and do not entertain a number of parasites who forget favors the moment they depart from my table.

Sept. 21. Returned from Brighthelmston to Bath.[1]

I cannot suffer a man of low condition to exceed me in good manners.

[1] Lord Chesterfield was at Bath at this time to try the waters, and writes to his son under date of Nov. 10, 1764: "The number of people in this place is infinite." See *Letters to his Son,* vol. IV, p. 207.

From Michaelmas [Sept. 29] 1764, the rent of my house commenced. The first year I am to pay but £110; but the second £120 per annum.

Nov. 11. My uncle Fred. was 70 years of age.

Every man has his price,[1] and the reason Sir Robert Walpole was so long in the opposition to the court, the minister did not come up to his price.

It was probably in reference to the celebrated struggle going on between the whigs and tories respecting the great American question, and perhaps under a severe twinge of the gout with which he was now dolorously afflicted, that the following caustic words dropped from his pen.

1765, Bath, March. The people of England are in general a set of hot headed fools; a parcel of senseless coxcombs who though perfectly able to examine the bottom of things, never judge farther than the surface. They know their rights and privileges are inviolably safe, and yet they are never easy unless they think them in danger.

Mrs. Mary Brooks at Angmaring near Arundel, Montham, good house maid.

The 25th of July is Bristol fair. About this time the Bath tradesmen settle their accounts and send in their bills.

1765, July 4. John M'Clester and his mother went to Bristol, Captain Osborne, bound to R. I.

Aug. 8. At Bath, degree of heat at 1 P. M. 76; at 7 P. M. 77.

---

[1] A favorite maxim of Sir Robert Walpole.

1766. Mr. Fred Frankland came to Bath Sept. 8th, and returned Oct. 24th.

1767 Tuesday, June 2, came to Hartham.

By $\frac{1}{5}$ of 88: interest paid Lady Frankland on 288, interest and principal £17 12*s*. By $\frac{1}{4}$ of £182 8*s*. to Fred Frankland, principal and interest on his legacy left by my father, £45 12*s*.

1768 Though Frankland left Lisbon in 1763, he continued to hold his office as consul general of Portugal until the summer of 1767,[1] when the king appointed Sir John Hort[2] in his stead, who remained at that lucrative post for many successive years.

His style of living at Bath may be inferred from the following schedule of his domestic expenses near the close of his journal.

My sister's calculation of annual charges in house keeping, viz., kitchen expenses, as food, soap, starch, blue and candles at £7 per week is £364; wages and livery of a coachman and two footmen at £20 each. £60.

Wages of three maid servants,	30.
Three coach horses,	100.
Wheels, £6 tax for do.	10.
Twenty chaldron of coals,	40.
House and taxes,	100.
Clothes and pocket money for Lady F. and self.	250.
Brewer's bill,	13.

---

[1] See *Boston Evening Post*, August 31, 1767.

[2] I was visited by Sir John Hort, the consul, 1780. *Cumberland's Memoirs*, p. 45.

Two saddle horses,	60.
Wine 4*s*. per day,	73.
Accidentals, viz., doctors, apothecaries and sundry other articles not foreseen or ascertained.	100.
	£1.200.

Dec. 9. I had that day been confined to my bed 14 weeks.

This is the last entry with date in the journal: his chequered life was now rapidly drawing to its close, and under the kind ministrations of his estimable lady, and sustained by Christian hope, he expired January 11, 1768, aged 51 years, 8 months and 1 day.

His remains were buried at the church in the beautiful village of Weston, near Bath, where the inscription to his memory by his excellent lady may be still read.

Through the kindness of Miss T. T. Whinyates, grand niece of Sir Charles Henry Frankland, a very pious and accomplished lady, still living at Cheltenham, England, I have been able to obtain a copy of the inscription, as well as a fine portrait of the baronet taken in early days. Under date of July 1859, she writes: "It is a very singular circumstance that the tomb of Sir Henry Frankland has been discovered by a mere accident by our cousin, Captain Frankland, R. N., who a few weeks since went to visit the tomb of a sister who lies buried at Ireston church in the vicinity of Bath. While there, he stumbled against the tomb of Sir Henry, not knowing in the least that his great uncle was buried there. He found that the monumental inscription was placed so very high against the wall in the nave of the church that it could not be well decyphered, therefore he requested that a copy might be made for him which is the same I now send you."

"To the memory of Sir Charles Henry Frankland of Thirkleby in the county of York, Baronet, consul general for many years at Lisbon from whence he came in hopes of recovery from a bad state of health to Bath, where after a tedious and painful illness which he sustained with patience and resignation becoming a Christian, he died 11th January 1768 in the 52 year of his life without issue and at his own desire, lies buried in this church. This monument is erected by his affectionate widow Agnes, Lady Frankland."

Of sound and discriminating judgment, good executive ability, accomplished manners and graceful mien, Sir Charles Henry Frankland seems to have performed his public duties faithfully, and even to the acceptance of the opposition parties. His political moderation and integrity secured the confidence both of whig and tory; and his aversion to political life and intrigue saved him from the calumniations which were unsparingly hurled against the heads of the very best men holding office in those stormy times. His mild and pensive cast of mind led him to take delight in the study of elegant literature; in observing the beauties of nature, in the practice of landscape gardening, in social converse and in religious meditations; and in his beloved Agnes, refined and beautiful above her sex, he ever found the liveliest sympathy and the most cordial assistance in his favorite pursuits. As a husband, he was ever affectionate, faithful and forgiving; as a friend and neighbor, generous and kind; as a citizen he was upright and noble; as a public servant, loyal, and as a Christian, we may hope that the penitence and prayer of his later, atoned through the blood of Him that cleanseth from all sin, for the delinquencies of his earlier years, and that to the golden gate of paradise he brought

"The gift that is most dear to Heaven."

CHAPTER XVIII.

Lady Frankland returns to America — Her occupation — Public sentiment — The arrest — The release — Battle of Bunker Hill — Return to England — Her second marriage — Death — Character — Mementos.

1768. Soon after the death of her husband, Lady Frankland, together with Henry Cromwell, for whom she ever cherished a fond regard, returned to this country[1] and in company with her sister, Mrs. Swain, formerly Mrs. M'Clester, her sister's children and other intimate friends and connexions, continued to reside on her beautiful estate at Hopkinton in her usual style of magnificence, until the opening of the great drama of the American revolution in 1775.[2]

She occupied herself in overseeing and directing the management of the farm, ornamenting the grounds with choice shrubs and flowers from Europe; entertaining the clergymen who occasion-

---

[1] The notice of their arrival is thus given in the *Boston Chronicle*, for June 13, 1768: "The Lady of the late Sir Harry Frankland, came passenger with Captain Freeman who arrived here last week from Bristol. The ship was the Juno, Captain Constant Freeman." See Drake's *History of Boston*, p. 742.

[2] The Province rate of Lady Frankland at Hopkinton for 1770, was for personal property, £3, 4*s*. 1d. Henry Cromwell's poll tax, 3*s*. 4*d*. See *Mass. Archives*, vol. 130, p. 749.

ally officiated at the Episcopal church, and some of her former friends, as the Amorys, Inches, Deblois, Ervings, etc., from Boston.

Surrounded, however, by a people ardently devoted to the cause of freedom, her position as the rich widow of a prominent officer of the crown; her devotion to the Episcopal church, and her splendid equipage, rendered her residence in the country every day more and more dangerous and perplexing. Liberty and equality had come to be the watchword of the times; the friends of England were at first suspected, and then at length declared to be the enemies of America. The arrival of armed troops at Boston, and the action of the liberty-loving patriots, Otis, Adams, Hancock, Warren and their noble compeers, finally rendered it necessary for the royalists to abandon their estates and betake themselves to flight. Leaving, therefore, her sister, Mrs. Mary Swain and her daughter, Mrs. John Dupee and family, in charge of the mansion and estate in Hopkinton, Lady Frankland and Henry Cromwell with a few trusty servants set out for Boston, early in 1775, in order to return to England.

She had taken the precaution to obtain permission of the continental congress to remove a small portion of her goods, with her to the city; but such was the excitement of the republicans against the loyalists at that remarkable period, that her carriage was stopped on the way to Boston by a party of armed men under the direction of Mr. Abner Craft, and her goods and person held in custody.

On the journal of the committee of safety of the provincial congress we have preserved the following interesting record in relation to this affair.

"May 15, 1755. Upon application of Lady Frankland, voted that she have liberty to pass into Boston with the following goods and articles for her voyage, viz; 6 trunks: 1 chest: 3 beds and bedding: 6 wethers: 2 pigs: 1 small keg of pickled tongues: some hay: 3 bags of corn: and such other goods as she thinks proper," and the following pass was then granted.

"To the Colony Guard.

Permit Lady Frankland of Hopkinton with her attendants, goods and the provisions above mentioned to pass to Boston, with the express order of the Committee of Safety.

BENJ. CHURCH, Jr., Chairman.

Head Quarters, Salem, May 15, 1775."

As Mr. Craft in his laudable anxiety to serve his country had captured the lady without regard to the instructions of the committee of safety, he was immediately ordered to appear before the provincial congress to answer to the allegations made against him in respect to the detention of Lady Frankland, and the congress, nobly jealous of its rights, then "resolved that he should be gently admonished by the president, and be assured that the congress were determined to preserve their dignity and power over the military."

"Mr. Craft was again called and the president politely admonished him agreeably to the resolve of congress." It was then resolved more favorably "that Lady Frankland be permitted to go into Boston with the following articles, viz:—seven trunks, all the beds and furniture to them: all the boxes and crates: a basket of chickens and a bag of corn: two barrels and a hamper: two horses and two chaises and all the articles in the chaises, excepting arms and ammunition: one phaeton, some tongues, ham and veal, sundry small bundles, which articles having been examined by a committee from this congress, she is permitted to have them carried in without further examination."

May 19. On the next day, so intent was congress in maintaining its supremacy over the military power, it was "resolved that Col. Bond be and hereby is directed to appoint a guard of six men to escort Lady Frankland to Boston with such of her effects as this congress have permitted her to carry with her and Col. Bond is directed to wait on Gen. Thomas[1] with a copy of the resolves of this congress."

Two brief autograph letters of Lady Frankland to this congress still remain. "The beauty of the graceful writing," says Mr. Wm. Lincoln, "is marred by many errors of spelling, showing that the defects of early education had not been all supplied." [2]

Defended by a guard of six soldiers Lady Frankland entered Boston about the first of June, then

---

[1] General John Thomas died of small pox at Chamblee, Canada, May 30, 1776.

[2] See the *Worcester Magazine*, January, 1843, p. 9.

in the possession of the British troops, amounting to about 12,000 men under the command of Generals Howe, Clinton and Burgoyne; was cordially greeted by her old friends, especially by General Burgoyne whom she had known in Portugal, and here from the windows of her elegant mansion on Garden-court street she witnessed, in company with many others, the imposing drama of the Battle of Bunker Hill, and aided with her hands to assuage the sufferings of the wounded from the bloody field.

Attended by Henry Cromwell, she soon after sailed for England, and resided in the Frankland family until 1782, when she was married to John Drew, Esq., a wealthy banker of Chichester. Her life, however, with him was brief; for taking a sudden cold, and inflammation of the lungs ensuing, she died, April 23, 1783, at the age of 57 years and was buried at Chichester. Raised from obscurity to affluence and high position in society, Lady Frankland's native good sense enabled her to fulfill the duties of her station with superior ability, while the radiant beauty of her person and the grace and dignity of her manners held dominion as by enchantment, over the affection of her husband, and shed lustre on the elevated circles in which it was her lot to move.

Her majestic gait, her dark and lustrous eye commanded the admiration of the beholder; her clear and melodious voice, her endearing smile entranced his heart. Her weight at the age of thirty-five, was about 136 lbs. Her chief amusements were reading, riding on horseback, music, and the culture of flowers. She was a communicant of the church of England, and in later life was highly respected and esteemed by the noble family into which she had married.

A few memorials of Lady Frankland still remain. Mrs. Aaron [Bixby] Reed of Norfolk, Va., a granddaughter of Isaac Surriage, has still in her possession a rich, striped silk brocade dress, — the green, purple and other tints beautifully interblending, — which once adorned the person of her great aunt Agnes. She has also a silver pepper box and milk pitcher on which the names "Frankland, Surriage and Bixby" are inscribed; a china cup which Lady Frankland gave to her brother Isaac Surriage on his going to sea; four silver teaspoons, one of which is inlaid with gold, and a copy of *Sir Charles Grandison* with her autograph on the title page. A most elegant and elaborately carved fan, on the folds of which is most exquisitely painted the coronation scene of George III, and which bears the name of Agnes Frankland, is still in the possession of the Porter family of Medford, Mass., where Mrs. Swain, in her later years, resided.

These curious relics which are held as very precious by their owners; together with the shrubbery and trees which her fair hands planted at her manor house at Hopkinton, are almost the only mementos that remain of a lady whose life was as romantic and eventful as any which the pen of the novelist has portrayed, or the fancy of the bard conceived.

CHAPTER XIX.

Henry Cromwell—The estate at Boston—Mrs. Sarah Swain—M'Clester—Isaac Surriage—The estate at Hopkinton—Dr. Shepherd—Mrs. Hildreth—Mansion burned.

Henry Cromwell entered the navy soon after his return to England, and was with Admiral Kempenfelt,[1] in the gallant action off the French coast on the 14th of November, 1781. He was held in high esteem in the navy, and rose to the rank of Captain, but being unwilling to fight against his native country, he retired from the service previous to the close of the Revolution. He was still living and had a family in Chichester in 1796.

On the decease of Lady Frankland, the estate in Boston came by will to her sister, Mrs. Mary Swain, from whom it passed into the hands of her son, Daniel M'Clester, who in a will bearing date, Medford, Aug. 1, 1807, devised it to his uncle, Isaac Surriage of Hopkinton. While in possession of the family, the estate was rented to various individuals,[2] among whom were Messrs. Bixby, Capen, Stoddard and Dr. Redford Webster, the father of Professor John W. Webster, who was hung for the murder of Dr. Parkman, Aug. 30, 1850.

---

[1] Lost in the *Royal George*, which went down at Spithead, Aug. 29, 1782. His age was about 70 years.

[2] Occupied by Alvin Fosdick and Nahum Fay, and valued at 3500 in 1798. See *Direct Tax*, vol. 7. The Hutchinson house was then valued at $5000.

Mr. Surriage disposed of the place, Sept. 30, 1811, for the sum of $8000 to Josiah Ellis, Esq., merchant, who repaired it thoroughly and continued to reside in it till his decease in 1829. The house was torn down about the year 1832, and the panels containing some beautiful landscape views were sold at auction and fell into the hands of Dr. Winslow Lewis of Boston. A large picture of the building itself, which in early times was second only to the famous Hutchinson house, is now in the possession of Mrs. Henry Ellis Dawes of the same city. Let such mementos of colonial times remain.

Lady Frankland's sister Mary, of whom frequent mention has been made, was married, first to a Mr. M'Clester by whom she had three children, viz: Daniel, Sally and John. Sally, born in 1740, was brought up in the family of her aunt Frankland and was married to Mr. John Dupee, a mathematical instrument maker in Boston, Nov. 3, 1757. On the death of Mr. Dupee, his widow, a large, gay woman, removed with her only son, Henry Frankland Dupee, born 1762, to the manor house in Hopkinton where he studied medicine with Dr. John Wilson of that town. He married Abigail Fairbanks, Aug. 7, 1785, and, soon after the Frankland place was sold to Dr. Timothy Shepherd in 1793, removed with his wife, mother and grandmother Swain to Dedham, and thence to Portland, Me., where, after a few years of successful practice, he died March 25, 1811, aged 49, leaving a son John and two daughters, one of whom married a Mr. White of Boston.

Mrs. M'Clester was married a second time to a Mr. Swain, whom she survived many years. Her son Daniel M'Clester married Sarah, daughter of George Stimson, Jr. of Hopkinton. She was born in 1759, and died of the small pox at the Frankland place in January, 1793, and was buried alone in the forest beyond the meadow in front of the house, where her solitary grave may still be seen. She left one child only, who died at the age of 14 years.

Lady Frankland's youngest brother, Isaac Surriage, for whom she entertained during life the tenderest regard, married Ruhamah Pedrick of Marblehead, Sept. 5, 1768, and having followed the sea for many years, at length settled in Hopkinton where he purchased a farm of 67 acres of John Parker, April 22, 1794, and where he died in Sept. 1813.[1] He left one daughter, Jennie, who was born in Marblehead, January 27, 1773. She was a great favorite of her aunt Frankland, whom she is said to have closely resembled in person, and with whom she spent many of her early days.

She was married to Mr. Pelatiah Bixby of Hopkinton, by whom she had Mary Swain, Edward Surriage, Hannah Webster, John Adams, Simpson, Susan A., Isaac Surriage, Caroline Agnes Frankland, and Charles P., and died Jan. 23, 1839.

Soon after Lady Frankland left Hopkinton, the estates of the loyalists were by an act of the provincial congress declared to be confiscate, and order-

[1] He lived in a small red house on the hill above Indian Brook. He afterwards bought the Rider and Tidd places. He was short, thickset and pitted with the small pox.

ed to be sold for the benefit of the state. In respect to the Frankland estate, the committee of safety and correspondence made the following report, May 24, 1766,[1] which shows us the condition of things at the house at that period.

"In compliance with your order of court dated April 3d, 1776, we the committee of correspondence, safety and inspection for Hopkinton, have in our opinion found a large estate, both real and personal of Lady Frankland, forfeited; but finding so many encumbrances on said estate, viz., Mrs. Swain, sister of Lady Frankland, and Mrs. Swain's daughter and grandson, and three negro slaves of which one is old and blind, we therefore pray that your honors would take it into your consideration and inform us how to proceed further."

In reply to this, the court say that "the resolve of the 19th of April last gives sufficient direction for the conduct of the committee of safety," and therefore the estate remained unforfeited. It continued in the hands of Mrs. Swain, Mrs. Dupee and her son until the year 1793, when it was sold by Rufus Green Amory,[2] Esq., attorney for Henry Cromwell of Chichester, Eng., to whom it had been devised by will of Sir Charles Frankland, to Dr. Timothy Shepherd of Sherburne for the sum of £950.

---

1 *Mass. Archives*, vol. 154, p. 52.

2 Son of John and Catherine Amory, and was born Dec. 20, 1760; was graduated at H. U. 1778, studied law and resided on Beacon street, Boston. He died May 15, 1833. See *N. E. Hist. and Gen. Register*, January, 1856.

Dr. Shepherd[1] dying in 1803, left the estate to his widow, Mary, a lady of uncommon beauty and accomplishments, who afterwards was married to Gen. William Hildreth of Dracut.[2] Left soon again a widow, this lady continued in possession of the estate until her decease, June, 22, 1857, at the advanced age of 87 years. The estate, reduced to about 100 acres, afterwards came into the possession of the writer, who had the misfortune to lose by an accidental fire on the 23d of January, 1858, the fine old mansion around which so many delightful associations clustered. Another building[3] similar in form and size and style has been erected on the spot; but nothing can repair the loss of this venerable mansion of the colonial times, whose rooms and closets, from the dark cellar to the capacious attic; whose folding doors with their huge iron fastenings, whose echoing halls adorned with Corinthian pillars, and with the beautiful tapestry of that period, brought up to mind so vividly the eventful history of those "celebrities," whose merry voices echoed here in days gone by.

But all is not yet lost. The well constructed

---

[1] Rep. from H. 1800-3. His children were Anne, married John Keyes, Esq., Nov. 27, 1816; Elizabeth, married Abijah Stone; Hannah, born March 3, 1794, married Charles Leland; Edward, born Nov. 9, 1796; Alicia, baptised May 4, 1799, and married Dr. Isaac W. Milliken, Nov. 17, 1825.

[2] Married April 17, 1809, and had one daughter Adaline, married Joseph Goulding, April 19, 1832. Mrs. H. received a pension of $325, until her death.

[3] Now occupied by Edward S. Nason, Esq., born at this place, May 10, 1820. Married Josephine C. Taft, July, 1850.

double walls of stone which still enclose the grounds; the terraces upon the sloping hill side; the blocks of skillfully wrought sand-stone on which the granery stood; the lines of box[1] in the flower garden, now some ten or twelve feet high; the avenue formed by Persian lilacs, now grown into noble trees; the snow-ball, the buck-thorn, pear and apple trees scattered over the plantation; the lofty and majestic elms[2] that wave their huge branches over the capacious green, falling by gentle inclination to the road:—these still remain, attesting to the wealth and taste of the original proprietor.

---

[1] The box is glistening high and green;
Like trees the lilacs grow,
The elms, high arching, still are seen;
And one lies stretched below.

Agnes, by Dr. O. W. Holmes.

[2] Within my memory there were seven magnificent elms standing in a line north and south, and shading the lawn on the west of the house. The one at the north was prostrated by a high wind several years ago, but is still living; the three at the south have been replaced by young trees. Of the three yet standing, the two outermost measure 12 feet in circumference, the one between them 9 feet and seems like a tall and slender sister rising up in stately beauty, claiming their protection.

CHAPTER XX.

Slaves — Hannah, Robert, Dinah — The Brands — Jennie Surriage — Dick Potter — Julia.

Frankland had upon this place, some twelve to sixteen negro slaves, who according to the custom of the times, were held in easy bondage, and who were set at liberty soon after the decision of the celebrated Lechmere case in 1770, which virtually put an end to the inhuman system of slavery in Massachusetts.

Among his slaves were Hannah and Robert who were with him at Lisbon; Dinah and Cato. Robert, or "daddy Bobby," as they used to call him, was a special favorite in the family. He shared the dangers of the earthquake with his master, and returned to Hopkinton, where he lived as a kind of fossilized relict from the other world until he became entirely blind, and finally died in second childhood. He was a genuine son of Africa, of inky blackness; he had the brand of the letter C, imprinted on each side of his body. He continued to wear his tarnished livery and to powder his white and crisped locks until his death.

An aged woman, who had but too many reasons for remembering him, informed me that she once in sport bit off one of the silver buttons of his coat; when he, though blind, caught hold of her and with his thumb broke out two of her front teeth. To make amends for this, she used, with Jennie Surriage, to powder his woolly head with Indian meal, ever taking good care to keep out of the reach of his cyclopean arms.

Dinah was also brought from Guinea; her face was jet black and she had been branded with three parallel lines upon the cheek and forehead. She was originally caught in Africa, as she herself used to aver, by means of a lump of sugar soaked in rum which drove her strength and reason out of her. She had several promising children, all of whom were born and baptized in the Frankland house. One of her sons bore the name of Richard or Dick, Potter, and obtained a world wide reputation for his feats of legerdemain. He attended school, when a lad at Hopkinton, obtained a pretty good education, and finally went with Mr. Skinner of Roxbury to reside in England, where he acquired the magical arts so perfectly and performed them so dexterously as to distance by a long interval every American competitor. Many persons still living can well remember his marvelous exploits in frying eggs in his new beaver; taking living rabbits out of gentlemen's coat pockets; or thrusting a sword, even to the hilt, into his own capacious throat and drawing out thence yard after yard of party colored ribbons and then spouting forth, to the astonishment of every beholder, sparks and flames of fire. In a very pleasant poem, John G. Saxe thus alludes to him and his performances.

I recollect the nervous man,
  Within whose hat the great deceiver,
Broke eggs as in a frying-pan,
  And took 'em smoking from the beaver;
I recollect the lady's shawl,
  Which the magician rent asunder,
And then restored; but best of all,
  I recollect the ribbon wonder.

I mean, of course, the funny freak
  In which the wizard, at his pleasure,
Spins lots of ribbons from his cheek,
  Where he had put 'em at his leisure;
Yard after yard of every hue
  Came blazing out, and still the fellow,
Keeps spinning ribbons red and blue
  And black and white and green and yellow.

I ne'er shall see another show,
  To rank with the immortal POTTER'S;
He's dead and buried long ago,
  And others charm our sons and daughters:
Years, years have fled, alas! how quick!
  Since I beheld the great magician:
And yet I've seen the ribbon trick
  In many a curious repetition. etc.

Potter died at an advanced age, and is buried at Andover, N. H., where he spent the last few years of his life. He left something of an estate to his descendants.

A daughter of Dinah, born in March, 1775, and bearing the name of Julia Titus, was living in 1860 in the full enjoyment of her faculties. She was a servant of Mrs. J. Dupee until the age of 17, could read and write, and from her I have derived many incidents relating to the slaves in the Frankland family.

Dinah's other children were Villot, who lived with Dr. Shepherd,[1] Phebe, Sidney and Robert. They were all mulattoes and very bright.

---

[1] July 10, 1794. "Primus Dr. to cash paid Mr. Dupee 6*s*. 3*d*." Dr. Shepherd's *Manuscript Journal*. His servants at this time were Primus, Julia, Cato, Pomp, Issacher and Vilot [Violet]. Cato received £20 per annum.— *Id*.

CHAPTER XXI.

The anniversary — Ghost stories — Origin — Echoes — Last visit to the mansion — Spirit of the present age.

When Frankland returned to Hopkinton after his wonderful escape from the earthquake in 1755, he brought with him the red broadcloth coat[1] which I have already spoken of as bearing the marks of the agony of the young woman buried with him, together with some other relics of that eventful day, and hung them along the tapestried walls of one of the chambers of his mansion.

On every anniversary of his deliverance from the dreadful catastrophe, he entered this room, locked the door upon himself, closed the shutters, and here in darkness and in silence spent the day in fasting, humiliation and prayer. The tremendous scenes of Lisbon were again recalled to mind, thanks again rendered for his salvation from the grave, and vows of faithfulness to Agnes and to God renewed. It was perhaps, owing to the dismal associations connected with this solitary chamber, together with the uniform tradition that a French boy had been murdered

---

[1] Where hung the rapier blade he wore,
Bent in its flattened sheath;
The coat the shrieking woman tore
Caught in her clenching teeth.

Agnes, p. 29.

This coat was afterwards made into one for Henry Frankland Dupee. [Mrs. A. Reed.]

on the farm and thrown into an old well in what was called "Hobb's Orchard," that the place had acquired the uneviable reputation of being haunted by the spirits of the departed. Often in my early days have I listened with greedy ear to the marvelous stories of "ghosts and goblins grim" which had been seen to stalk forth from the lonely woodlands in the dusky twilight, causing every heart to quake with fear. It was said, and more than half believed, that an apparition in white had often been seen wandering near the solitary grave of poor Mrs. M'Clester; that the headless trunk of the murdered French boy used to appear gliding along the border of the forest just when the shade of evening became deep enough to render objects indistinct; that low, sepulchral moans were heard; that the pump in front of the house had been observed to work by the influence of some invisible hand, and *horresco referens*, — to spout forth torrents of blood; shrieks of murdered children had been heard from the walls of the building at the solemn hour of midnight, and a troop of horse with manes and tails on fire and nostrils breathing flames had terrified the people by capering and prancing over the grounds amid the darkness and the violence of the winter storm.

The loneliness of the situation, the primeval woods of Magunco, where a tribe of Indians once lit up their watch-fires, and where the owl still startles the nocturnal traveller by her hootings; a remarkable echo[1] which seems in the stillness of the evening to come directly from the well where the poor French boy is supposed to have perished; the memory of the revelling, the wassailing which once resounded through the tapestried halls of the mansion; the strange, romantic fortunes of its inmates, all conspired to favor the idea that these supernatural agents still returned and wandered in the night time around these old domains as their most favorite haunt; and when I last revisited that venerable mansion, from which the sacred remains of its long, last occupant had just been carried to the grave; walked through the lonely and silent rooms, observed the tapestry loosely hanging from the deserted walls; the columns of the capacious, but now empty hall; as I passed through the "haunted chamber"[2] where the spoils of Lisbon earthquake used to hang, and stood upon the very floor on which the English baronet had so often kneeled in penitence and prayer; as I recalled to memory the fair maid of Marblehead and her romantic story; as I with busy fancy repeopled the whole scene with forms of beauty and intelligence, listened to the sounds of the merry viol, of song, of feasting and of revelry; saw Frankland, Agnes, Harry Cromwell, Isaac Surriage,

---

[1] This echo repeats distinctly such phrases as *Vox præterea nihil*, etc., and is best heard a few yards south of the large elm tree nearest the road. Another fine echo is heard on the plateau in front of the house and still another on the hill above.

[2] This was the middle chamber on the south side of the house.

Dupee, Villiers, the Prices, Wilsons, Valentines, Ervings, groom, footman, waiter, valet, page, Robert, Hannah, Dinah, all alive before me,—and as I then paused and looked again and saw the rooms deserted and the shades of evening falling, and heard no sound save the echoes of my own solitary footsteps, I confess that it required but little effort of the imagination to believe that invisible spirits were still hovering around me, and that the weird fancies of the boy had become realities to the man.

But the sharp, shrill whistle of the steam engine speeding up through the valley by Magunco dispels the reverie. It is the voice of this wonderful age we live in, telling us that the days of romantic adventure and of gibbering ghosts are over; that the wigs, the ruffs, the gold-laced coats and the wassail bowls; the love knots and the courtly dames; the armorial decorations and the prestige of the Shirleys, the Auchmutys, the Hallowells, the Apthorps, the Franklands, and the Hutchinsons, have long since gone by; that the fetters of colonial servitude are long since broken; that the blessed beams of liberty now irradiate alike the cottage of the poor, and the mansion of the wealthy; and that, from abject dependence on foreign domination, we have now come to be a vast, consolidated people, illumined by the lucid ray of science, elevated by the light of religion, exulting in power, and marching onward in the front rank of the nations, buoyant with hope, towards a destiny too exalted even for the pinion of fancy to reach.

FINIS.

INDEX

TO

NAMES OF PERSONS AND PLACES.

www.ingramcontent.com/pod-product-compliance
Lightning Source LLC
LaVergne TN
LVHW021417110826
845150LV00007B/1972

* 9 7 8 1 4 2 5 5 0 9 7 6 7 *